Fulfilling a Vision

Fulfilling a Vision

The Contribution of the Church of Scotland
to School Education, 1772–1872

JOHN STEVENSON

☞PICKWICK *Publications* · Eugene, Oregon

FULFILLING A VISION
The Contribution of the Church of Scotland to School Education, 1772–1872

Pickwick Publications
An Imprint of Wipf and Stock Publishers
199 W. 8th Ave., Suite 3
Eugene, OR 97401

www.wipfandstock.com

ISBN 13: 978-1-61097-344-1

Cataloguing-in-Publication data:

Chia, Edmund Kee-Fook.

Fulfilling a vision : the contribution of the Church of Scotland to school education, 1772–1872 / John Stevenson, with a foreword by William Storrar.

xviii + 170 p. ; 23 cm. Includes bibliographical references and index.

ISBN 13: 978-1-61097-344-1

1. Scotland—Church History—18th Century. 2. Scotland—Church History—19th Century. 3. Scotland—Social Life and Customs—18th Century. 4. Scotland—Social Life and Customs—19th Century. I. Storrar, William. II. Title.

BR785 S800 2012

Manufactured in the U.S.A.

Cover Illustration by Douglas C. Stevenson

Seeing that God hath determined that his Kirke here in earth shall be taught not by Angels, but by men; and seeing that men are borne ignorant of God and of all godlinesse, and seeing also he ceases to illuminat men miraculously, suddenly changing them as he did the Apostles and others in the primitive Kirk; Of necessitie it is that your Honours be most careful for the vertuous education and godly upbringing of the youth of this realme.

—The First Book of Discipline (1560)

Contents

In the Path of John the Commonweal

THE HISTORY OF SCOTTISH education is inseparable from its relationship with the Church in Scotland. John Stevenson tells his important and controversial chapter in this story with scholarly insight, balanced judgment and compelling narrative skill. As the Church of Scotland and other mainline Protestant churches in North America, Europe and Australasia face the challenge of shrinking membership and resources, as well as internal divisions, it is all the more important that we heed John Stevenson's spirited account of how a Reformed Church kept alive its vision of a well educated society in the nineteenth century, a period of equally profound economic and social change, and fierce denominational rivalries. Stevenson inspires us to maintain our theological commitment to the common good of all in education, even in these hard times for our churches.

In truth, it has always been 'hard times' for the Church and education in Scotland, with never enough resources or qualified teachers to make this vision a reality for all. In the years before the Scottish Reformation in 1560, many voices called out for the reform of Church and nation to create a more just society. The most powerful attack on corruption and plea for spiritual renewal in late medieval Scotland came not from a clergyman but from a prominent diplomat at the royal court, Sir David Lindsay of the Mount. His play, *A Satire of the Three Estates*, exposed the follies and failings of the nobility, bishops, and merchants of Scotland. In a unique way, it departs from the conventional genre of medieval morality plays, with their stock caricatures of the virtues and vices, by bringing on to the stage a real poor man of the time called John the Commonweal. This Everyman exposes the neglect of true religion and the welfare of the poor by Scotland's leaders in the three estates of the realm, and pleads the cause of Christian reform in church and society. His case is predicated on his ability to read the New Testament for himself and quote it back to the bishops with telling effect. John the Commonweal is the literate lay voice of Christian humanism in late medieval Europe; an advocate of reform whose eloquent plea for an educated laity is echoed by Erasmus in his own satire of religious and political corruption, *In Praise of Folly*. Scotland before the Reformation was a cultured northern European nation, with schools in the towns, three universities founded in the course of the fifteenth century, and an even older tradition of sending its finest students abroad to study and teach in continental universities. Scottish education produced a remarkable line of eminent scholars of international reputation, including Duns Scotus, next to Thomas Aquinas perhaps the greatest thinker of the medieval era, and John Major, the teacher of both John Calvin and Ignatius Loyola at the University of Paris.

As in the rest of Europe, the origins of this Scottish educational tradition lie in the Church and its mission to found schools and universities for the edification of the people and the professional needs of society; all to the glory of God, as the Biblical mottos of two of the three oldest Scottish universities founded by Papal Bull at St. Andrews (1411), Glasgow (1451: *Via, Veritas, Vita*) and Aberdeen (1495: *Initium Sapientiae Timor Domini*) remind us. Having taught in two of these ancient universities, and latterly in their late born Protestant sibling in Edinburgh (1583), it is a particular honour to write the Foreword to such a fine study of the contribution of the Kirk to education in the nineteenth century. John Stevenson has written a modern chapter in an ancient story.

The story of Scottish education at its best is the story of John the Commonweal—an egalitarian and later democratic vision of educating ordinary people to read God's word and live in its light, and to seek wisdom in all spheres of secular human inquiry: the practical and the philosophical, the scientific and the social. No one did more to institutionalize that egalitarian vision of education than John Knox in the mid-sixteenth century, with his call for a school in every parish. John Knox is an enigmatic figure in Scottish and world history. The leader of the Scottish Reformation, Knox was lionized in the centuries that followed as the pioneer of universal education, only to be demonized in our more secular age as the poisoned source of an oppressive cultural

Calvinism. This Knoxian paradox is everywhere evident in our public life and literature.

While the educational experience of some in Calvinist Scotland undoubtedly was cruel and unkind, this is to miss the point of Knox's lasting legacy, a vision of secular and religious education for all social classes, as John Stevenson ably demonstrates in this book.

Let me make that point from my own educational experience. Growing up in the Scotland of the 1950s and 1960s, I lived through the last decades of the nineteenth-century settlement described in this book, where the primary (elementary) and secondary (high) schools were publicly funded and administered, open to all, and yet deeply infused with the religious practice and moral ethos of Protestant Christianity. Two teachers stand out in my personal memory and gratitude but they are representative of a much wider pedagogical practice in Scotland. Miss Elizabeth Armstrong was my teacher in the final year of Primary School. Samuel Stevenson was my English teacher and debating coach at High School. Betty Armstrong toured the continent of Europe on a scooter, and crossed Canada by train during the summer vacations, bringing us back colour slides of her exotic travels, a benign Miss Jean Brodie, opening up vistas on the wider world to village children, while teaching us to write and think and paint, and recite poetry and sing songs in our native Scots language, the language of Sir David Lindsay and John the Commonweal. Sam Stevenson taught generations of working class adolescents to form our own arguments, think critically, and venture out with confidence into the national public arena, while introducing us to opera, symphony concerts, and plays. Both Betty and Sam were stern disciplinarians, devoted teachers, and devout Christians, pillars of their local churches. This is Knox's educational legacy at its best in Scotland, not dour and demeaning for its children but life enhancing and liberating. As John Stevenson enables us to see so clearly, through all the twists and turns of educational politics in the mid-nineteenth century, this is what the Church of Scotland and its education committee were trying to achieve in the remoter Highland and rural regions of the country, as well as in its poorer and industrializing Lowland communities—a vision of national education with the parish church at its heart.

But something did change in the relationship between the Church and education in Scotland after 1872, as this book also explains. The person who first pointed out that sea change to me was another John, John McIntyre. He was an eminent Scottish theologian of the second half of the twentieth century, Professor of Divinity and Principal of New College and twice Acting Principal (President) of the University of Edinburgh during vacancies to that high office in Scottish education. There could not be a more distinguished modern representative of the Scottish Reformed tradition in education than Professor and Principal McIntyre. Two conversations with him stand out in my memory.

While doing research on church and nation in Scotland, I interviewed John McIntyre on the secularization of Scottish society in the course of the twentieth century, and its impact on the Kirk. He wondered aloud in our conversation whether the Church of Scotland's biggest mistake in response to modernity was to give up its parish schools with the education act of 1872. With the steepening decline in Kirk membership and growing indifference to organized religion in Scotland from the later 1950s onwards, McIntyre thought that it might have been better for the Kirk to hold on to its day schools, and therefore its wider influence on the youth of Scotland beyond its own ranks, like the Catholic Church in Scotland and the Church of England south of the border. Whether McIntyre was right or wrong in that tentative thesis, and this book offers fresh insight on his characteristically astute speculation, his comment shows the continuing importance of education to the life and witness of the Church, even in more secular times.

My second educational memory of John McIntyre is from the time when he was acting Principal and Vice Chancellor of the University of Edinburgh. As it happened, I had the privilege of sitting on the Court, the governing body of the university, with McIntyre at the meeting that confirmed the controversial appointment of the first Catholic holder of the historically Reformed chair of theology at New College. After the meeting, John McIntyre leaned over to me and whispered, "We had to appoint him. He was the best candidate." This comment by McIntyre shows another vital trait of Scottish education at its best, fostered by the Kirk before and after the Reformation. As John Stevenson argues, education from primary school to university had not only to be democratic and open to all. It also had to be meritocratic and open to the best talents, irrespective of denominational affiliation.

I write this foreword from Princeton in the USA, where I now direct an advanced research institution after parish ministry, school chaplaincy, and university teaching in Scotland. When I arrived here, I found a statue of a fellow Church of Scotland minister, the Reverend John Witherspoon, waiting to greet me on the campus of the neighbouring Princeton University. As President of the College of New Jersey in the later eighteenth century, Witherspoon became one of the most influential educators during the American Revolution. He was the teacher of the future President James Madison, and a host of other leaders in the young republic, and a signer of the Declaration of Independence. Standing far back in the shadow of this great Scottish American, I am reminded by John Stevenson that we followed the same Scottish path to Princeton, the historic Reformed educational highway from village school to high school and on to university and parish ministry, there to encourage the next generation on the same road. It is an educational course that Presbyterian Scots have exported around the world, not only to the United States and Canada but also to Africa, Asia, Australasia, and Latin America. That is why this national study of the Church of Scotland and secular education is of much wider interest and merits an international readership, not least among Church and secular educators around the world.

Here then is the story of Scottish education and the Church, exemplified in this foreword by John the Commonweal and John Major in the medieval era, and after the Reformation by John Knox, John Witherspoon, and John McIntyre. And now we have John Stevenson, in his own right a distinguished exemplar of that same Scottish educational tradition. After parish ministry, he served as General Secretary of the Education Department of the Church of Scotland, where he guided the Kirk in its concern for the schools, colleges, and universities of Scotland, and the educational welfare of its children, youth, and adults. This John is uniquely placed to write this timely study of the work of his own education committee in the nineteenth century. He has carried its vision faithfully into our own time. It is a vision of the educational mission of the Church we must renew for future generations.

William Storrar
Center for Theological Inquiry
Princeton, NJ

Preface

THIS BOOK BEGAN AS PhD thesis that I was originally encouraged to undertake by Stewart J. Brown, Professor of Ecclesiastical History in the University of Edinburgh. As a parish minister I had been involved in school education for many years but it was my work as General Secretary in the Church of Scotland's Department of Education that allowed me to pursue my interest in the field of state education. The Education Committee whose work in the nineteenth century this book describes is the Church of Scotland's longest continuing standing committee. Today it still speaks for the Church on matters of state education. Realising the respect in which the committee has been held by politicians and educationalists I considered it worthwhile to write about its early achievements, pioneering as it did school inspection, teacher training, and the establishment of new schools in the industrial Lowlands and in the less accessible Highlands and Islands of Scotland. The story is one of conflict and dispute often centring on the place of faith and religious teaching in schools. Then as now education was subject to political policies and pressure. The Education Committee of the Church had to remain true to its goal of raising the standard and availability of a good inclusive education and yet hold on to its conviction that denominational religious instruction had to be part of the curriculum. What eventually emerged was a system of state controlled education and yet one in which the contribution and advice of the church was welcomed. In the early 1980s the Church's Education Committee brought to the General Assembly the findings of a special working group set up to examine the aims of education. Its Report, "A Good Education," was important in determining the future approach of the church. It concluded that "the supreme aim of education is the fostering of right relationships . . . this is more important than the commonly stated objective of the fullest development of individual capacity. What is needed is to give young people the chance to develop their talents for the good of all . . . both religious and moral studies are an integral part of the stuff of everyone's education." This, I believe, would still be the Church's position today. It is certainly in tune with what the church sought to achieve in the nineteenth century and echoes the sentiments of the Scottish Reformers that education should help to develop the individual's talent and that this should be for the "commonweal." I hope that the reader will be as fascinated as I am in seeing how the issues raised in the nineteenth century are still matters of contention today be it the provision of funding, the standard of teaching, the breadth of the curriculum, targets and attainments, the place of religious and moral education, or questions about faith schools.

While most historians writing about nineteenth-century Scotland do mention the Church of Scotland's involvement with school education, none have dealt at any length with the activity of the Education Committee. Writers who have contributed to the discussion have mainly concentrated on the debate over the introduction of a national system of education in Scotland and on the Church's desire to hold on to its control of parish schools. R. D. Anderson, Donald J. Withrington, and others have offered valuable contributions to our understanding of school literacy and attendance, the supply of schools, the effects of government legislation, and the part played by the various denominations in this period.[1] It is evident that what is missing is a fuller explanation of the Church's aims and objectives in all this. This book aims to offer a more detailed account of the working of the Education Committee and of the policy adopted by it, and to present the Church's actions and achievements in a more positive light than hitherto has been the case.

Professor Brown was always happy to advise me and his wide knowledge of Thomas Chalmers and of British history in the nineteenth century greatly assisted me in my research. For a number of years I have enjoyed the friendship and advice of Dr. Andrew Bain who is the author of several studies on Scottish school education during this period. Our discussions have always been stimulating and productive. I am grateful to Dr. William Storrar for agreeing to provide a Foreword and to all who have encouraged me to write this book. In particular I must express my thanks to my wife, Mairi, who through good times and difficult times would not allow me to give up.

---

1. Anderson, *Education and the Scottish People*; Withrington, *Going to School*.

Abbreviations

AGA	*Acts of the General Assembly of the Church of Scotland*
NAS	National Archives of Scotland, General Register House, Edinburgh
OSA	*Old Statistical Account of Scotland*
PP	Parliamentary Papers
SSPCK	Society in Scotland for Propagating Christian Knowledge

Unless otherwise stated "Church of Scotland" is taken to refer to the Established Church of Scotland.

Introduction

There is room for doubt whether the tradition which speaks so highly of old-time Scottish education had any basis in fact, except in a parish here or there.[1]

THE FIRST BOOK OF *Discipline* drawn up by John Knox and his fellow reformers has a chapter entitled "For the Schooles" in which is set out a nation-wide scheme for the establishment of schools closely associated with the parish churches. It was Knox's great vision that there should be a school in every parish and that a basic education should be available to all so that even the poorest child would at least be able to read the Bible. It was also his hope that young people with potential who might be the future leaders of society should follow a course of education that would take them to university. Knox's proposals were in line with an approach to education which had already been established in Scotland. The Medieval Church was not only a religious and social institution but also a great educational institution. The "Sang Schools" within the abbeys and monasteries not only trained future monks and provided choristers for the choirs, but many offered a basic grounding in reading and writing. In addition to this there were schools attached to cathedrals and to collegiate churches. Later, to cope with the population growth in the new towns, classes were held outside the ecclesiastical precincts. These "outer schools" were the first Grammar Schools. At the same time as "outer schools" were being developed monks were sent out to teach children in the towns and the burgesses began to provide accommodation and payment for this. Gradually town councils took over responsibility for these schools.

As the burgher class of tradesmen and craftsmen grew in number so this created a greater demand for these "outer schools" and for the education of children within the town itself. In places like Edinburgh,

1. Campbell, *Two Centuries of the Church of Scotland, 1707–1929.*

1

Haddington and Arbroath schools which were probably originally intended for the training of future monks and priests came to be used to meet the educational needs of the sons of the nobility and gentry. An Act of 1496 ordained that all barons and freeholders of substance should send their eldest sons and heirs to school from the age of eight or nine and then afterwards to university for three years, a twenty pound fine being imposed on any who failed to do so. This Act confined education to a certain social class nevertheless it is significant that one of the earliest laws regarding education to be passed in Scotland should carry with it the note of compulsion and that this compulsion should extend beyond elementary schooling to university or college education. The Reformers therefore inherited the framework of an educational system—monastic and burgh schools, and three universities.

By 1560 almost all the burghs of any size in Scotland had a grammar school. Apart from these burgh schools before 1560 schools were neither numerous nor necessarily permanent. The mention of a school in early historical records is no evidence of its continuous existence. In 1567 Parliament agreed that the Church had a right to approve all teachers in parish and burgh schools and in all universities and colleges. At the same time the General Assembly of the Church of Scotland granted commissions for the planting of schools in some of the Highland parishes (Inverness, Ross, Caithness, and Sutherland) but funding was short and progress was slow. Assemblies and Kirk Sessions in these first years after the Reformation were probably too busy re-establishing parish churches and recruiting ministers to give much time to schools. It was the seventeenth century before Parliamentary and General Assembly legislation concerned itself with the establishment of schools.

By the mid-seventeenth century the Kirk had settled a minister of religion in almost all of the nine hundred parishes in Scotland with the exception of some parts of the Western Highlands. With schools it was a different story. Lack of finance on the part of the Church and lack of interest on the part of Parliament and the Scottish Lords had hindered any real attempt at the application of Knox's ideal.

During the seventeenth century the Scottish Parliament did legislate for the setting up of schools. The 1633 Act, Ratificatioun of the Act of Counsall anent Plantatione of Schooles, ratified the Act of Privy Council of 1616 regarding the establishment of schools and gave bishops the power to assess land for taxation purposes for the establishment and maintenance of the schools. This was the first attempt to lay the financial burden upon the local landowners—the "heritors."[2] This Act was strengthened by the Education Act of 1646 which ordered locally funded, Church-supervised schools to be established in every parish in Scotland and again by the 1696 Act for Settling of Schools. The General Assembly of the Church of Scotland had also been anxious to encourage the establishment of schools but its voluntary contributions were quite inadequate so it expected libraries to be set up and schools and schoolmasters to be paid for out of local taxation or by landowners as the legislation required.[3] From the middle of the seventeenth century the Church regularly passed Acts of Assembly appealing to Parliament to implement the existing legislation for the planting of schools and the provision of funding but it was always a struggle to make heritors pay up. While presbyteries had the responsibility of supervising schools and local ministers in cooperation with the heritors could examine and appoint schoolmasters, since the initial provision of schools and the payment of schoolmasters was the responsibility of the heritors the future of parish school education largely rested with them. In 1704 the Church made an abortive attempt to fund its own schools. The General Assembly passed an *Act Anent Erecting Schools in the Highlands* and agreed that presbyteries and synods should endeavor to collect subscriptions and contributions "for erecting schools and educating youth in the Highlands and Isles." It also recommended that presbyteries and synods[4] should send to the Commission of Assembly an account of what "Paroches have or want Schools, and what places do most need them." In 1705 the Assembly passed an *Act concerning Schools and Bursaries, and for instructing Youth in the Principles of Religion* in which it ordained that ministers should "take care to have schools erected in every Parish, conform to the Acts of Parliament, for teaching Youth to read

2. Scottish landowners who had legal obligations and responsibilities such as the upkeep of roads, the payment of the parish minister and schoolmaster, and the maintenance of the church and the school. In a series of Acts of the Scottish Privy Council and Parliament in 1616, 1633, 1646, and 1696, it was laid down that heritors in each parish should be responsible for the maintenance of a school and the schoolmaster's salary.

3. AGA Session 9 on March 22, 1703, and AGA Session 10, March 27, 1704.

4. The Church of Scotland has a Presbyterian structure, which means it is organized under a hierarchy of courts. Traditionally there were four levels of courts: the Kirk Session (at congregational level), the Presbytery (at local area level), the Synod (at a regional level) and the General Assembly (the Church's highest court). However, the synods were abolished in the early 1990s as they had ceased to have any significant power.

English." There is no indication that any schools were erected from funds collected. It would appear that such funds as were gathered were eventually handed over to the Society in Scotland for Propagating Christian Knowledge which was set up in 1709. The Church very soon discovered that for all its desires and resolutions to extend school education it could do little by itself.

In spite of its early ideals and ambitions the eighteenth century saw the Church demonstrating a considerable disinterest in schooling. Presbyteries were inclined to neglect what powers they had to inspect and examine schools. A decline in social morality and fear of the doctrines of the French Revolution, however, awakened the Church from its complacency and there was a growing anxiety at the lack of schools and the poor conditions of schoolmasters. It was not until 1824, however, that the Kirk's General Assembly considered that the answer might lie in the Church setting up its own schools.

The committee which embarked upon this task the following year was appointed in the first instance out of a concern for the educational needs of the Highlands and Islands of Scotland. After initial success funding proved the great stumbling-block to any scheme which would have made any real impact on the deficiencies of the existing system of education. The first programme for training teachers was developed but this too was costly and by 1834 it had become clear that the Education Committee could not expand its work without the help of government grants.

By the early 1840s an incredible variety of persons and agencies had become involved in setting up schools in an attempt to meet the needs of Scotland's youth—for example, as well as Assembly schools set up by the Church of Scotland, there were parish and burgh schools, privately endowed schools, schools run by the Society in Scotland for Propagating Christian Knowledge, an increasing number of schools run by the Glasgow Catholic Society, and over two thousand adventure schools[5] which, in general, provided the poorest instruction by the least able teachers in the land. To this state of things must be added the explosion of Free Church schools following the Disruption in 1843. There was no central body to manage or co-ordinate this multiplicity of educational establishments and no way of planning to meet the needs of the new industrial towns where the old parish school system could not function. The growth of

5. Schools founded "on the master's own venture"; that is, set up by private individuals on their own initiative and at their own expense.

new schools meant an increased demand for government grants and with this demand came the argument that all denominations should be treated equally in the distribution of state funds. It was these factors, aggravated perhaps by the Free Church's resentment of the Established Church's privileged position with regard to the parish schools, which convinced many that there was a need to establish a national non-denominational school educational system in Scotland. A succession of government bills attempting to devise such a scheme were vigorously opposed by the Established Church which refused to relinquish its control of parish schools and which argued that with its parish schools and with its Assembly schools to supplement these, Scotland already had a manageable national system.

In implementing its education programme in the nineteenth century, the Church believed that it was fulfilling an obligation that had been passed on to it by Knox and the Reformers. The Church believed that its responsibility for schooling was enshrined in legislation going back to the sixteenth and seventeenth centuries and ratified in the Acts of Union which had confirmed the Church of Scotland as the Established Church and laid down that all schoolmasters had to be members of it.[6] On the basis of this legislation the Church claimed a statutory right to examine and superintend all Scottish schools and to ensure that young people were given a "godly upbringing." In its role as the protector of education the Church of Scotland was jealous of any rival and suspicious of any changes that it did not itself initiate. Whenever it felt its position threatened, either by political events, as at the time of the French Revolution, or by other denominations or by government legislation, it cited Parliamentary and General Assembly Acts to affirm its authority and endorse its claims. In establishing its new schools, the Church saw itself as supplementing an existing system of national education for which it had a statutory managerial responsibility. In its published statistics the committee always included parochial schools[7] as "Church of Scotland schools."

These convictions, however, ultimately brought the Church into headlong conflict with politicians who sought to change the system and

6. Following the 1689 Act of Settlement, which brought William and Mary to the throne of the United Kingdom, an Act was passed in 1690 establishing the Presbyterian system of Church government in Scotland. The status of the Presbyterian Church of Scotland as the "Established Church" was confirmed in the Acts of Union 1707.

7. "Parochial" is the old form of "parish." Throughout we shall normally use "parish" and "parish schools."

with successive governments on which the Church became increasingly dependent for financial aid.

By 1872 the Church had successfully planted 286 schools in different areas of the country with teachers supported from a central fund gathered largely from congregational givings. It had, moreover, endeavored to improve professional teaching standards by insisting that teachers should be trained and by co-operating with the government's scheme of school inspection. Just as important, its work had inspired Kirk Sessions and local industrialists to establish schools in some of the most deprived areas of Scotland's cities. In 1871, by including twelve hundred parish schools, the Church claimed responsibility for a total of 2,430 schools throughout the country.

By this time, however, there was a growing majority both in church and state who believed that further expansion of school education would only be possible if the management and funding of schools was centralized in a Scottish Board of Education. This was accomplished in the 1872 Education (Scotland) Act. State control meant that the contribution of the Church was no longer needed or possible and gradually the Church's schools and other subscription schools were handed over to local authorities. This book charts the contribution of the Church of Scotland to the development of Scottish school education over the hundred years leading up to the 1872 Act.

1

A Duty Neglected

THE WANT OF SCHOOLS

A T ITS MEETING IN Edinburgh in May 1824, the General Assembly of the Church of Scotland was persuaded that the situation with regard to school education in many parts of Scotland was critical and agreed to consider the need for a special committee to tackle the problem. It reached its decision mainly on the basis of figures drawn from a government survey published in 1818 by Henry Brougham who had been appointed by the House of Commons to report on "the charitable establishments for education in Great Britain." For the purposes of his report Brougham had asked the General Assembly in 1818 to circulate a number of questions to all parish ministers in Scotland with a view to establishing an accurate estimate of the educational provision in Scotland and an Assembly committee under the convenership of George Baird, Principal of Edinburgh University, was set up to undertake this task. The questionnaire sent out asked for the population of parishes, the number who had not been taught to read, and whether or not the parish school was situated where it could be conveniently accessed by children from every end of the parish. In the course of this investigation it came to light that the Society in Scotland for Propagating Christian Knowledge (SSPCK), whose work was so essential in the Highlands and Islands, had been turning down applications for new schools and closing down some of its existing schools, due to shortage of funds.[1] Some seven hundred returns were received from ministers

---

1. The Society in Scotland for Propagating Christian Knowledge had been founded in 1709. By 1714 it had established seventeen schools and by 1808 some thirteen and a half thousand pupils attended SSPCK schools.

and passed on to Brougham who later returned them to Baird.[2] The statistics which were presented to the General Assembly showed that certainly by the early nineteenth century there were large tracts of Scotland where there was little or no educational provision. Brougham's enquiry recorded 942 parish schools in Scotland, but the inadequacy of even that number to meet current needs was, according to Baird, demonstrated by the fact that it was being supplemented with 2,222 adventure schools.[3] The accuracy of Brougham's figures and conclusions was questioned by the Aberdeen researcher Donald Withrington[4] who was of the opinion that the English clerk appointed to collate the statistics for Scotland had difficulty applying Scottish terminology to the classifications which had been prepared for England. Certainly the observations made by the parish ministers in their returns showed just how varied the picture was throughout the country. In the County of Aberdeen alone the difference between parishes is striking. For example it was reported that in Aberdour the parish school was small and in a ruinous condition and in Crathie Braemar the school was totally unfit to meet the needs of the parish. On the other hand the parishes of Macher and Bourtie could boast that the schools were adequate and that all the children were taught to read and most of them could write and count. In the County of Argyll schooling was said to be sufficient in only three out of the thirty-two parishes, while in the County of Dunbarton in ten out of twelve parishes the means of education was described as sufficient even for the poorer classes.

Many of the problems highlighted by Brougham's report had been long-standing. In 1696 the Act for Settling of Schools had made it the responsibility of the heritors in every parish to provide a school and the salary of the master. Where they refused the Act gave powers to presbyteries to appeal to the Commissioners of Supply[5] who would then establish the school and pass on the cost to the heritors. Almost seventy years later, however, in 1758 the SSPCK reported to the General Assembly that, in spite of this legislation, within the bounds of the thirty–nine presbyteries where the Society had erected charity schools, some 175 parishes out of

---

2. It is estimated that there were 938 parishes in Scotland at this time.

3. These were schools set up and taught by individuals and paid for out of pupils' fees.

4. Withrington, "The SPCK and Highland Schools," 88–89.

5. The unelected precursors of County Councilors. They had the responsibility of collecting local taxes and representing the county landholders.

a total of 380 were still without parish schools.[6] As a solution the SSPCK had recommended that the Assembly should instruct every presbytery in Scotland to conduct a survey to determine which parishes had schools. The SSPCK also reiterated its threat to withdraw its schools from those parishes where no parish school had been provided claiming that it was not the job of that organization to do the heritors' work for them and substitute their Charity schools in place of parish schools. The Society had made the same complaint in 1749. At that time it had forcibly expressed its criticism of presbyteries which, it claimed, for some time had neglected to visit schools and had made no effort to enforce those Acts which required heritors to make provision for school education in each parish. Instead the Church had become totally dependent on the schools established and paid for by the Society. These complaints and threats would appear to have had little effect. Four years later the matter was again before the Assembly. In 1762 a committee which had been appointed to consider a reference to the building and repairing of kirks and manses, and the setting up of schools where there was a need, recommended that the Assembly should instruct presbyteries to carry out those Acts of Parliament which made provision for the building and repairing of churches and for establishing schools. It also suggested that a committee should be appointed to oversee this and that presbyteries should report back to the next Assembly. The Assembly agreed to these recommendations but it is doubtful if any were ever carried out. There is no account of any reports from presbyteries in the proceedings of the following Assembly. It would be the last years of the century before such a procedure would be followed.

Other sources of information available to the Church describe the same diverse and inconsistent picture. In spite of the SSPCK's criticisms of heritors in the minutes of heritors' meetings there is considerable evidence that at least in some areas many were attentive in the upkeep of school buildings and the appointment of schoolmasters. Even where the heritors themselves were not always present they appointed representatives to attend meetings and speak for them.

The *Old Statistical Account* (*OSA*)[7] had revealed that while the provision of schooling over the country was patchy there were some striking

6. These presbyteries were mainly in the Highlands. This was only about half of the presbyteries there were in Scotland at that time.

7. The *Old or First Statistical Account of Scotland* was compiled by Sir John Sinclair from information submitted by the parish ministers who had been invited by him to

examples of what was available. The small parish of Kiltearn (Ross and Cromarty) with some 1,616 inhabitants, for example, could boast of a parish school which taught Latin, French, geography, geometry, and mathematics to some sixty to eighty children, while a town like Paisley claimed to have an English school in each of its three parishes, a grammar school, a school for teaching writing and arithmetic, and several private schools. On the other hand the parish minister at Forbes and Kearn in Aberdeenshire claimed in his report that there never had been a parish school in that district. There were, however, many schools other than parish schools. Apart from adventure schools and subscription schools, there were a growing number of Charity schools. By the middle of the eighteenth century Edinburgh alone had four Hospital schools—Heriot's, the Merchant Maiden, the Trades Maiden and George Watson's. In addition in many of the major towns Burgh or Grammar schools had long been established and offered an extensive curriculum which included more scientific and practical subjects as well as the classics. In 1746 the Town Council of Ayr had adopted a scheme for a Grammar School teaching a wide range of subjects including Latin, Greek, natural philosophy, geometry and algebra. A similar Academy was opened in Perth in 1761. One of the ministers in the parish of Elgin reported that the magistrates and influential citizens planned to set up an academy in the town which would include mathematics, book-keeping and land-surveying in its curriculum. On the whole the portrayal of school education in the *OSA* is not so much a want of schools as an education system deteriorating as a result of poor salaries and the lack of properly trained and qualified schoolmasters. While there may have been some kind of school in the majority of parishes the need for more schools was recognized particularly in the remoter areas of the Highlands where distances made school attendance difficult.

The consensus view of historians today would appear to be that opportunities for elementary education in Scotland at the end of the eighteenth century and into the early years of the nineteenth were not as scarce as Brougham's calculations made out. Scottish academics such as T. C. Smout and R. D. Anderson have taken the view that by the end

---

describe their parishes in detail. The etymology of the parish name, its natural resources, climate, industries, population size, a descriptions of its churches and, eventually, schools, were among the details requested. A complete copy of this publication in twenty-one volumes was presented to the General Assembly in May 1799.

of the eighteenth century there was a basic network of schools which could have been described as a national system.[8] This was certainly the case in the Central Lowlands of Scotland. An examination of the 1818 returns bears this out. Parishes such as Dundee, Paisley, Renfrew, Port Glasgow, Dumbarton, Linlithgow, and Clackmannan were all reported as being able to provide access to schooling for even the poorest classes. It has to be remembered, however, that not all children of school age attended even where schooling was available. In his *Digest*, for example, Brougham's calculations showed that out of a population of 1,805,688, only 176,525 children were attending school, and many of those for only part of the day. About one in ten fell into this category. Moreover the geography of the Highlands and the poverty of the people meant that for many children living there at that time there was little or no chance of attending school. To this must be added the fact that the situation in the towns was deteriorating as can be seen from the statistics provided by the *New Statistical Account* (*NSA*, 1834–1845). It would appear that in one parish in Glasgow (the Barony) at the end of the eighteenth century most of the people had been taught to read and write but the number fell drastically as the density of the population increased and by 1850 out of 592 children only ninety-nine were attending any school.[9] Indeed Smout concluded that the provision of elementary education worsened for most members of Scottish society in the half-century beginning around 1780 due to the shift of population from the countryside to the towns.[10]

THE ROLE OF THE CHURCH ESTABLISHED BY LAW

The duties of presbyteries and kirk sessions had been clearly set out in Acts of the realm and in General Assembly instructions going as far back as 1565 when the Assembly claimed as a right that "none be permitted to have charge of Schooles, Colledges, or Universities, or yet privately or publickly to instruct the youth, but such as shall be tryed by the Superintendents or visitors of the Church," and found to be able and sound in doctrine. This claim was ratified by an Act of Parliament in 1567.[11] Here the reference to the Church's power to examine teachers in

8. Anderson, *Education and the Scottish People*, 4 and 14; and Smout, *A History of the Scottish People*, 425.

9. Compare *OSA*, vol. 12, with *NSA*, vol. 6.

10. Smout, *A History of the Scottish People*, 443.

11. 'Anent thame that salbe Teicheris of the Youth in Sculis,' in *Booke of the Universall Kirk of Scotland* I: 60, 108. In 1706 the Assembly passed an Act recommending that

"all scules to Burgh and Land" and to its responsibility for the instruction
of youth "privatlie or openlie," is worth noting. The Church believed that
its powers of superintendence applied to all schools but it is evident that
it saw itself also as part of a partnership. In 1645 the General Assembly
passed an Act which stated that all schools, including burgh and grammar schools should be visited twice a year by inspectors appointed by
presbyteries and town councils.[12] These visitations were intended to ensure the provision of a high standard of school education and of suitably
qualified schoolmasters. The Church, through the presbytery or parish
minister, could exercise a large measure of control over the appointment
of masters and their assistants, but in burghs the town council exercised
an administrative control in such matters as school hours, vacations, the
curriculum, repairs and equipment. This superintending power of the
Church was established by the Treaty of Union in 1707 and was confirmed by a number of succeeding Acts. Of course, as might be expected,
there were times when the jurisdiction of the Church was questioned
and when cooperation between the Church and the town councils broke
down. In November 1775 Dunfermline Town Council decided to remove
the master of the Grammar School. This was unanimously opposed by
the Kirk Session of Dunfermline Abbey who were perfectly satisfied with
his ability and his conduct and claimed that since they paid part of his
salary they had at least an equal say in his appointment. In the end the
Session (apart from the Moderator) agreed to undertake a re-trial of the
schoolmaster along with representatives from the Town Council. And
there was always someone who took exception to a session being involved
with schooling in this way. When Dunfermline Abbey Kirk Session was
considering setting up a Sabbath Evening School one of the elders, a Mr
Thomson, complained and stated his belief that the Kirk Session had no
power to establish either public or private schools or to giving anything

---

"Presbyteries do visit all Public Grammar Schools within their Bounds" at least twice
every year (*AGA*, 1706, 10–11).

    12. *AGA* 1645. *Overtures for the advancement of Learning, and good Order in
Grammar Schools and Colledges.* "Every Grammar School be visited twice in the year
by Visitors, to bee appointed by the Presbytery and Kirk Session in Landward Parishes,
and by the Town-Councell in Burghs, with their Ministers; and that no School-Master
be admitted to teach in a Grammar School, in Burghs, or other considerable Paroches,
but such as after examination, shall be found skilfull in the Latine Tongue; And that after
other trials to be made by the Ministers, and others depute by the Session, Town, and
Paroch for this effect, that he be also approven by the Presbyterie."

out of the public funds to support schools this being the responsibility of the magistrates. In spite of these differences of opinion the Church held to its position and felt confirmed in its beliefs by the fact that Grammar schoolmasters and Towns Councils often invited presbyteries to carry out examinations of their schools.

How far schools were in fact visited and examined by the local ministers or kirk sessions in the eighteenth century is difficult to discover. The existence of statutory and Assembly legislation enabling presbyteries and kirk sessions to examine schools did not by itself guarantee their implementation. Church records show that a fairly attentive supervision in the seventeenth century fell away during the eighteenth century. While the minutes of heritors' meetings describe their efforts to provide school buildings and schoolmasters' salaries and their decisions to appoint teachers whose qualifications had been examined and approved by kirk sessions, with regard to any inspection of schools the kirk session records are silent. The main involvement of kirk sessions seems to have been helping to pay for the education of poor children out of the Poor Fund and in augmenting the schoolmaster's salary by appointing him as Clerk or by putting him in charge of the Sunday school. The minutes of Cramond Kirk Session for June 1797 reveal that paying for the education of poor children was such a strain on its resources that it could only keep them at school for three years in order to give other children the opportunity of attending. The Kirk Session of Montrose Old for its part decided that the best way to deal with poor children was to erect a "working school" or "school of industry" where these children could be trained to read, knit, card, and spin, and "thereby instead of being burdens on their Parents and Pests of Society to be useful to both."[13]

When we turn to the role played by Presbyteries the picture is equally depressing. While presbyterial superintendence of schools had long been established what was not clear was how exactly it was to be done and what it was supposed to cover. What is missing from church records is any suggestion of regular routine visits to schools. In most cases where presbyteries were forced to make better provision or to discipline teachers action was only taken in response to problems or complaints raised by heritors or parents or by schoolmasters themselves. In 1784 in Dornock it was left

13. While Spinning Schools were set up mainly in the Highlands by the SSPCK during the eighteenth century, industrial schools and female schools did not become a priority for the Church until the middle of the nineteenth century.

to the children's fathers to complain to Annan Presbytery about the lack of a schoolhouse, and when it was brought to the attention of the heritors they agreed to build one. Again it was the heritors and the families who in 1790 petitioned the Presbytery of Forfar to dismiss the schoolmaster at Inverarity for failing to fulfill his duties. In Langholm it was the heritors who asked the Presbytery to investigate the state of the school and complaints against John Telfer the schoolmaster accused of fornication and intemperance. Had presbyteries been doing their duty conscientiously they would have been the first to know about such problems and taken steps to try and resolve them. Writing about his schooldays Hugh Miller gives some useful insights into the involvement of parents: "Some of the wealthier tradesmen of the town, dissatisfied with the small progress which their boys were making under the parish schoolmaster, clubbed together and got a schoolmaster of their own; but though a rather clever young man, he proved an unsteady one, and, regular in his irregularities, got diurnally drunk . . . getting rid of him, they procured another."[14]

There were, of course, a number of exceptions to this pattern. In 1782 Turriff Presbytery visited the parish school at King Edward and examined the pupils in the books they had been reading and rebuked the master for not praying with his pupils before he dismissed them. At the request of the schoolmaster of Perth Grammar School the magistrates of Perth and representatives of the Presbytery met for the purpose of examining the students there. The minutes of Dundee Presbytery show that from 1780 Dundee Grammar School was being examined yearly and in March 1787 the Presbytery resolved to carry out yearly inspections of parish schools. Each year thereafter the minutes record reports of these visits. Also in 1787 Glasgow Presbytery appointed a committee to draw up a plan for putting into practice the intentions of the Presbytery with regard to the education of the city's children. Schoolmasters and teachers who had not already been certified as qualified were to be examined by the Presbytery[15] and each teacher was to provide the Presbytery with a list of all their pupils, an account of their

---

14. Miller, *My Schools and Schoolmasters*, 122. Hugh Miller (1802–1856) became famous in his lifetime as a writer and as a specialist in the field of geology.

15. Presbyteries were obliged to examine schoolmasters and teachers not only with regard to their academic ability but also to ensure that they were "qualified to Government," that is, that they had signed the Church's Confession of Faith (the "Formula") and taken the oath of allegiance to the Government.

progress, and an account of the catechisms taught. Attention was also to be paid to the morals and behavior of the children in each school. There is, however, no mention in subsequent minutes of any action being taken as a result of this investigation. When a minister who had been teaching in the school at Glamis was being considered for the post of schoolmaster there, the pupils for whom he had been responsible were examined on their progress in different subjects. Perhaps the best examples of presbytery supervision in this period are to be found in areas where the Society in Scotland for Propagating Christian Knowledge operated. As early as 1774 Glasgow Presbytery had appointed a committee to examine the SSPCK school established to meet the needs of the Highland families who had migrated to the city. In the Presbytery of Lewis many of the teachers there were also missionaries responsible for rural churches and mission stations. It seems to have been the case that these teachers were appointed and supervised by the Presbytery and were funded partly from the Royal Bounty[16] and partly by the SSPCK. (The political and cultural implications of the work financed by the Royal Bounty have perhaps not always been fully acknowledged. In his study of James Moore, a catechist on the island of Colonsay from 1728 to 1736, Dr Domhnall Uilleam Stiubhart has drawn attention to the fact that this new religious and educational initiative was designed to make the Gaels useful and obedient subjects of the British state, loyal to the Presbyterian church and to the Hanoverian succession, by weaning them away from the ever-present dangers of Jacobitism and by eventually wiping out the Gaelic language and culture. According to Stiubhart, these ulterior motives became plain when at the close of the 1725 General Assembly, the Church's Committee for the Reforming of the Highlands and Islands and the Management of the King's Royal Bounty had its first meeting and began the reorganising of the Highland presbyteries.[17] In 1797 the Presbytery of Lewis appointed committees to examine all the schools within their bounds including Stornoway

16. The Royal Bounty was money given each year by the Crown "for the reformation of the Highlands and Islands of Scotland for promoting the knowledge of true religion, and suppressing Popery and profaneness and superstition." In co-operation with the SSPCK it employed missionaries and catechists to go from house to house instructing people. In some instances it was used to help pay for schools and teachers.

17. Domhnall Uilleam Stiubhart, *The Colonsay Catechist*, a collection of serialised articles published in *The Corncrake*, the online magazine of the Island of Colonsay.

Grammar School. Instances of presbytery intervention such as these were, however, the exception. Normally after teachers were in place presbyteries do not seem to have checked up on standards of teaching or the performance of pupils until something went wrong. In the fifteen years prior to 1794 there are few references in presbytery records to indicate that a routine duty of visiting schools was actually undertaken. Too often presbyteries were used as trouble-shooters rather than as agents for promoting a good education. In an article in the *Records of the Scottish Church History Society* Archibald Main had this to say:

> The Church had failed to realize the ideal which it had set before itself since the days of John Knox. There was no uniform system of education throughout the parishes . . . the poverty of the Church and of many heritors in the eighteenth century, the social and economic circumstances of the era, a lack of imagination on the part of many ministers, some lukewarmness regarding the nobility of the teaching profession in the parish schools, and perhaps an undue regard for a narrow theological discipline—such were some of the considerations which prevented a widespread system of sound elementary education in every parish of Scotland.[18]

THE QUESTION OF AUTHORITY

However anxious the Church may have been to fulfill the duties of examining schoolmasters and visiting schools, its authority in the sphere of school education was always limited by the role of the heritors with whom they shared the responsibility of appointing schoolmasters and whose legal obligation it was under the Acts of 1646 and 1696, to provide parish schools and pay schoolmasters. As we have seen a similar division of responsibility existed in the Burghs where Town Councils managed schools and paid teachers but where the Church claimed the right of visitation and a say in appointments made. Given this sharing of jurisdiction it is no wonder that there was often disagreement about where ultimate responsibility lay and a questioning of the privileges claimed by the Church. Most of the arguments concerned the method of examining schoolmasters by presbyteries on their appointment and the power of Church Courts to discipline and dismiss them. The parish schoolmaster's security of tenure was a matter of considerable controversy in the eigh-

---

18. Main, "The Church and Education in the Eighteenth Century," 194.

teenth and nineteenth centuries as we shall see. Certainly teachers were emphatic in their support of this protection, it was one of the attractions of the profession. Others, particularly those responsible for the supervision of schools saw it as making it more difficult to get rid of incompetent teachers.

For much of the time heritors and presbyteries were to be found working together in the presentation of schoolmasters and the care of schools. Indeed, there were times when, as has been shown, heritors seem to have been more aware of the needs and problems of schools than presbyteries. There were, of course, other times when presbyteries and heritors clashed as happened when heritors were reluctant to provide the necessary funding for schools or for repairs to school buildings and stayed away from meetings called to discuss these matters. Those sections of the Acts of 1646 and 1696 which gave powers to presbyteries to put pressure on heritors to establish schools, may well have been difficult to implement by this time. In 1782 Forfar Presbytery sought the backing of the Procurator[19] when the heritors refused to attend a meeting to discuss repairs to the school at Inverarity. Here it was apparent that, while the Procurator gave his support to the Presbytery, as so often proved to be the case the Presbytery's powers to compel the heritors to do anything were very limited and in this instance the Presbytery had to seek the support of the Commissioners of Supply. It is clear that on those occasions when the Church's Procurator was approached for a ruling or for support, he regularly expressed doubts about the power of presbyteries and passed the buck back to presbyteries for decision and action. As a result a case could be passed back and forth for years between heritors and a presbytery and between a presbytery and the Procurator. Always there seems to have been uncertainty as to where the final authority lay and the weakness of the Church's position when ignored or opposed by a civil body was apparent. The same was true even when a presbytery was challenged by an individual. In June 1777 Mr. Alexander Ramsay, a grammar-school master in Dunfermline, having taken the Oath of Allegiance refused to take the next step of subscribing to the Confession of Faith on the grounds that he considered himself teaching in a private school over which, he maintained, the Church had no jurisdiction since by law only parish schools could be examined. The Presbytery tried to dismiss Ramsay but when

19. The principal legal advisor to the General Assembly of the Church of Scotland.

he appealed neither the heritor, who was the Marquis of Tweeddale, nor the Procurator of the Church nor the General Assembly were prepared to make a firm decision one way or the other and the civil magistrates refused to become involved. In the end Ramsay himself foreclosed the matter as far as the Kirk was concerned by joining the Relief Church.

Perhaps one of the most famous cases of this period concerned the appointment of a schoolmaster to the school at Bothwell This highlighted not just the disputed roles of presbytery and synod but, even more significantly, the jurisdiction of the civil courts, in this case the Court of Session, in ecclesiastical affairs. The case which was first raised in September 1790 in the Presbytery of Hamilton, came about as a result of some members of that Presbytery questioning the qualifications of William Allan the newly appointed schoolmaster and the method by which he had been elected. When those who opposed Allan's appointment took their dispute to the Synod of Glasgow and Ayr, Allan protested that such an appeal was not competent on the grounds that according to the law, only presbyteries could examine a schoolmaster, and that it was not competent for a synod to review the proceedings of the Presbytery in this matter. The case eventually went to the General Assembly in 1791 where the Procurator passed it on to the Court of Session. In November 1793 the Court of Session gave a decision which deprived the Superior Church Courts of their jurisdiction in questions relating to the qualifications and character of parish schoolmasters. The Court of Session found that the power of review lay in the Civil Courts and not in the superior courts of the Church. On hearing this, the Synod immediately protested that this ruling was contrary to the law of the land and the Presbyterian government of the Church of Scotland upheld by the Treaty of Union. An appeal was then made by the Synod to the House of Lords and the ruling of the Court of Session was reversed. Although the matter was eventually found in favor of the Church, the case clearly highlighted the threat by public bodies to the Church's position in matters of school education.

Certain conclusions may be drawn from this overview of the Church of Scotland's involvement with school education over approximately two decades, 1774–1794. Firstly, while it is possible to cite examples of kirk sessions and presbyteries taking part in the appointment and disciplining of schoolmasters, few of the records describe attempts to carry out the long-standing Acts of the General Assembly regarding the supervision of schools in any other way. It would appear that presbyteries and kirk sessions were not fulfilling their obligations to visit and examine schools on a regular basis. When presbyteries did act this was often as a result of pressure from heritors or parishioners. Whereas the *First Book of Discipline* had required ministers and elders visiting schools to examine "how the youth have profited," few records indicate such an assessment being made. It may be that such duties were taken for granted and not thought worthy of reporting at meetings or recording in the minutes. On the other hand it could be argued that matters concerning education, which had been brought so often to the attention of the nation in parliamentary and church legislation, should have been important enough to report on and record. While this judgment perhaps needs to allow for the fact that there appear to have been no clear guide-lines as to what was expected of a presbytery's visitation of a school other than what was laid down by the *First Book of Discipline*, as a general conclusion it would appear to be supported by what has been discovered of the attitude adopted by those ministers who were influenced by the spirit of Moderatism. The weight of evidence points to a parish ministry not particularly suited or equipped for the task of examining schools. On a more positive note, it should be recognized that, at a time when standards seem to have been deteriorating, even the limited role exercised by some presbyteries in overseeing the condition of school buildings and in examining the faith and character of schoolmasters must have had a beneficial effect on Scottish school education. What the minutes do show is that where church courts, in particular presbyteries and synods, were involved in matters concerning schools, disputes often arose with regard to their rights and responsibilities. In the secular world there were growing doubts as to the power and authority of the Church.

THE INFLUENCE OF MODERATISM ON THE PARISH MINISTRY

One explanation of the apparent laxness of the Church with regard to school supervision may lie in the interests and values of a parish ministry influenced by the spirit of Moderatism and the Scottish Enlightenment.[20]

20. During the eighteenth century Moderatism gradually dominated the religious scene in Scotland. The Moderate wing of the Church supported "patronage"—the appointment of parish ministers by patrons, usually the local landowners. The marks of Moderatism were tolerance and the absence of dogmatism. Their ideal was a broad-based undogmatic Kirk which would be a source of moral improvement. Ministers who were Moderates were often accused of spending most of their time in worldly pursuits. They were opposed by the Evangelical or Popular Party, which stood for Calvinist orthodoxy,

It is difficult to avoid the impression that under the influence of the
Moderate Party and the Edinburgh literati the main educational interests
of Scottish churchmen in the second half of the eighteenth century lay
in upgrading and expanding university education and in the broad cultural improvement of society, rather than in parochial education *per se*.
Good manners, politeness, moral virtue and common decency were what
counted and what children learned at home was seen as of considerable
importance. For these ministers of the Kirk education should focus on
character formation and moral correctness rather than the imparting of
knowledge or the three R's.[21] This philosophy of education was hardly
likely to encourage an interest in the parish school with its traditional
curriculum and in the ongoing tasks and hardships of parish teachers in
the classroom. With this as the predominant contemporary attitude to
education it is more than likely that the involvement of parish ministers
and kirk sessions in schools declined and with it a corresponding diminu-
tion of the influence and authority of the Church in this field. It is worth
noting that of the five main movers among the Moderate literati (Hugh
Blair, William Robertson, Adam Ferguson, John Home, and Alexander
Carlyle) only Carlyle completed his schooling at a parish school, the
other four had a grammar school education. We cannot tell exactly what
influence their educational background may have had on how they saw
the importance of visiting parish schools in the course of their ministries and how this in turn affected the ministries of the many who sought
to emulate them, but it may have bred a notable indifference. Such an
approach to school education, moreover, cannot be attributed only to
those ministers who strictly speaking belonged to the Moderate party.
By the last quarter of the eighteenth century the differences between the
Moderate and the Evangelical parties in the Church were becoming less
obvious, at least as far as cultural and intellectual values were concerned.
J. G. Lockhart, the biographer of Sir Walter Scott and an acute observer
of his times, described the relationship of Moderates and Evangelicals in
his witty and illuminating portrayal of the General Assembly in *Peter's
Letters to his Kinsfolk*:

---

commitment to the parish ministry and Christian discipline and believed that church
members should have a say in the appointment of ministers.

21. See Dwyer, *Virtuous Discourse*, 77ff.

They [the Moderates and the Wildmen] stick with the most sena-
torial pertinacity, each to his own side of the Senate-house. . . .
I am at a loss to know what are the distinguishing tenets to which
they respectively adhere . . . so far as doctrine is concerned, the
two parties profess themselves to be agreed. . . . Were I to judge
from what I have observed in the General Assembly, I should
certainly be inclined to think that the attributes of *Wildness* and
Moderation, are by no means confined to the opposite sides of the
aisle . . . [They] may be seen, year after year, drawn up against each
other without having an inch of debateable land to fight about.[22]

The parish ministers who contributed to the *First Statistical Account*
reflected this common legacy of the Enlightenment in the way they approached their subject matter. In these volumes are to be found the interests of eloquent and eminently worldly-wise observers who often devoted
more space to long lists of population statistics, describing epidemics, the
etymology of the parish name and economic and agricultural developments than they did to recording the state of education and the condition
of the parish school. It is possible that they limited their accounts of the
educational provision to conceal their neglect of school supervision but
the fact that the first edition of the questionnaire issued by Sinclair omitted any reference to schools could not have helped. Referring to the ministers who contributed to the *Statistical Account*, the Scottish historian
T. C. Smout has remarked that, "one has only to turn the pages of that
remarkable compilation to see them come to life, not as pastors, but as
intelligent gentlemen sowing clover, speculating on ornithology, applaud-
ing a new linen work or a new road, agitated over the expense of poor
relief, nervous of the effect of rising wages on rural virtue and watchful
for any signs of idleness among the laboring classes."[23] We are left with the
impression that these parish ministers may well have been out of touch
with the needs and aspirations of their flock. In John Galt's novel *Annals
of the Parish*, Mr Balwhidder the minister is surprised to discover that
the new bookseller is ordering a daily London newspaper for the spin-
ners and weavers when he thinks he does well to get a newspaper twice a
week from Edinburgh.[24] The intellectual and social decline of the Scottish
Presbyterian clergy was acknowledged by several commentators during

22. Lockhart, *Peter's Letters to His Kinsfolk*, 31–37.
23. Smout, *History of the Scottish People*, 221.
24. Galt, *Annals of the Parish*; *The Ayrshire Legatees*; *The Provost* 69 and 104.

the last decade of the eighteenth century and the early nineteenth century. Describing Thomas Chalmers before his conversion Stewart Brown believed that he was typical of many clergymen who "regarded their parish as little more than a sinecure while they pursued eminence in other, academic, endeavours."[25] A contributor to the *Scots Magazine* in 1801 drew attention to the seriousness of the gap between pastor and people, which threatened the very future of a Church, claiming that with their "predilection for technical divinity and mystical rant" the clergy of the Established Church had lost touch with their congregations.[26] Henry Cockburn,[27] for his part, claimed that there had emerged two classes of clergymen, one whose only aim was to pay obsequious allegiance to the patrons and the other who had no taste or ambition for anything beyond what was necessary to minister to the lower classes. He concluded that "the descent of the Scotch clergy throughout the last half of the eighteenth century was steady and marked . . . not that there were no distinguished men among them; but there were not many, and they were always decreasing." In fact T. C. Smout has suggested that it was as the strict Calvinism and authority and influence of the Church declined in the eighteenth century that Scotland's cultural achievements flourished.

Certainly it would be wrong to give the impression that all Church of Scotland ministers at this time were totally removed from parish affairs. Alexander Carlyle[28] was known to excel as a preacher. He helped to establish a Sunday school in his presbytery, used his connections frequently on behalf of his parishioners, and was actively involved in the allocation of poor money and the administration of the poor house at Musselburgh. Without the leadership of men like Carlyle kirk sessions could not have operated as they did in looking after the needs of the people, be that in matters of discipline, in distributing funds to the poor or in allocating

25. Brown, *Thomas Chalmers and the Godly Commonwealth in Scotland*, 71.

26. J. P. G., "The Present State of the Clergy of the Church of Scotland." *Scots Magazine* 63 (1801) 389–92.

27. Lord Henry Cockburn (1779–1854), Scottish advocate and social and political commentator. The Cockburn Association was founded in 1875, in part to continue his campaigning to protect and enhance the beauty of Edinburgh.

28. Alexander Carlyle (1722–1805) was the minister of Inveresk Parish Church for fifty-seven years. During this time he became leader along with his historian friend William Robertson, of the Moderate party. Carlyle's friends included most of the Enlightenment figures including David Hume and Adam Smith. They called him 'Jupiter' Carlyle because of his imposing presence and love of classical learning.

burial plots. The extent of the parish minister's actual involvement with parish schools, however, remains uncertain. Many may have been unwilling to be involved in an area which could lead to a confrontation with heritors and landowners on whose financial support they depended. Reading Carlyle's own account of his life and ministry, one wonders just how much time he did spend visiting his parishioners since he seemed to be away from the parish so frequently. Certainly in his writing he said nothing about visiting schools. On the other hand a diary kept by Hugh Cuningham of Tranent, a contemporary of Carlyle, contains many references to faithful pastoral activities and records regular visits to the parish school and his examination of the pupils there. Any attempt to assess how Church of Scotland ministers actually saw their calling in the latter half of the eighteenth century, is not helped by the fact that contemporary commentators like Lockhart (1794–1854) and Thomas Somerville (1741–1814) tended to concentrate on the preaching and oratorical skills of famous city ministers, rather than describe the pastoral oversight of their parishes.[29]

From the available evidence it is apparent that we may form contradictory views of the parish ministry in this period. Someone like the twentieth century historian Andrew J. Campbell, who wanted to defend the clergy and the General Assembly, has provided a good illustration of these divergent opinions. He conceded that presbyteries and ministers often failed to carry out the General Assembly's instructions and that in all ecclesiastical parties there could be found ministers who were indifferent to the work of the ministry and enjoyed wining and dining but maintained that throughout the country there were some who were as dedicated and diligent as at any other time and that schools would have been in an even worse state had it not been for the Church's help.[30]

THE PLIGHT OF THE SCHOOLMASTERS

From all reports it is clear that it was not just a lack of schools that hindered the progress of school education in the second half of the eighteenth century, it was also the lack of good schoolmasters. Poor salaries and conditions were a discouragement to the recruitment of well-qualified men

29. See Lockhart, *Peter's Letters*, vol. 3, 38ff.; and Somerville, *My Own Life and Times*, 57–63 and 91–107.

30. Campbell, *Two Centuries of the Church of Scotland 1707–1929*.

and had contributed to a decline in the status of the parish schoolmaster. The General Appendix published with the *Statistical Account* included a "Memorial," drawn up for the parochial schoolmasters in Scotland in 1782 which presented a melancholy picture of their situation. It underlined the fact that the salaries of schoolmasters had not been increased in line with the general increase in wages nationally and made a passionate plea for salaries which would measure up to the importance of the work.[31] By 1785 Scottish schoolmasters themselves were organized enough to be ready to petition Parliament regarding their salaries and an edition of the *Scots Magazine* published that year described a meeting held in Edinburgh to discuss the next move. At that meeting, however, it was agreed to delay an approach to Parliament to allow time for further consultation with the heritors and royal burghs. Presumably the schoolmasters did not wish to take any action which would alienate those on whom they were dependent for their keep. In 1792 schoolmasters petitioned the Church to support their demand for a salary increase and there is evidence to suggest that at a local level some landowners recognized the schoolmasters' plight and increased their salaries and that kirk sessions encouraged teachers to charge higher fees for teaching new subjects such as French and geography.

In their contributions to the *Statistical Account* many parish ministers expressed their grave concerns for the future of schoolmasters. The minister of East Monkland parish made the point that the schoolmaster's salary, paid by more than a hundred heritors, was scarcely worth collecting, while the minister of Glasford parish in the Presbytery of Lanark maintained that the ploughman's wages had doubled over the past forty years past while the schoolmaster's condition in that time had undergone no material change for the better. Poor salaries meant that often schoolmasters were anxious to move on to acquire a better living. The account from Glasford commented that over six years there had been five changes of schoolmasters. For many it meant taking on other jobs. Teachers might be old soldiers, shopkeepers, auctioneers, postmen and even schoolboys. One teacher who was over seventy years of age was also precentor, session clerk, beadle and gravedigger while another augmented his salary from cock-fighting. While the Church was sympathetic it seemed that there was little it could do about the want of schools and the plight of

---

31. General Appendix to *OSA*, vol. 21, 336–41.

schoolmasters. Its hands were tied since the power to augment salaries lay with the heritors and not with the General Assembly. Into the bargain the stipends of ministers themselves at that time were also falling behind the increasing prosperity of the country and they were fighting, unsuccessfully, their own battle with heritors and the government for an augmentation.

It was the lessons of the French Revolution rather than the school situation which eventually forced the Church to call for government action. In 1799 with the threat of invasion hanging over the nation, the Assembly in its wisdom decided that schoolmasters were essential for safeguarding the morals of the people and upholding the Constitution. From what appears to have been this rather ulterior motive of protecting King and Country, the members passed "A Declaration and Instruction of the General Assembly in favor of the Parochial Schoolmasters in Scotland." This instructed the Moderator and the Procurator to take every opportunity to make the Church's concern for teachers known and to correspond on the matter with His Majesty's Officers of State for Scotland, offering to support any plan they might come up with for the relief of schoolmasters. On this occasion the appeal from the Assembly was listened to (presumably because the Government agreed with the Assembly that schoolmasters could be "effectual instruments" in the contemporary political situation) and the result was the *Parochial Schools (Scotland) Act* of 1803 (sometimes referred to as the Education Act).[32] This Act almost doubled the schoolmasters' salaries by raising the minimum to three hundred merks[33] (approx. £16) and the maximum to four hundred merks (approx. £22), these rates to continue for twenty-five years.[34] It laid down that where there was no schoolhouse, one consisting of two rooms and a garden was to be provided by the heritors. Where parishes were extensive or divided by the sea it was competent, but not obligatory, for the heritors to set up two schools and divide the salary between the two schoolmasters, thus establishing what came to be known as "side schools." For all this the heritors had to provide the additional funding. The superintending du-

32. An Act for making better Provision for the Parochial Schoolmasters, and for making further regulations for the better Government of the Parish Schools in Scotland. 43 Geo III, c 54.

33. The *merk* was originally a Scottish silver coin worth about one shilling but its value varied over the years.

34. The average salary in the 1790s was about £8.10s.

ties of presbyteries and ministers were restated, and although the Church
was to continue examining schoolmasters the heritors could decide on
the extent of this examination and so control the curriculum. It could be
said, therefore, that this Act actually reinforced the power of the heritors,
and to that extent it lessened the power and authority of the Church. The
main weakness of the Act was that it applied only to the existing parish
set-up and failed to take account of the educational needs of the rapidly
expanding population in the burghs and urban areas.

THREATS AND FEARS

It will be evident from what has been said that towards the end of the
eighteenth century all was not well with school education in Scotland
and that there were problems with the Church's dealings with it. There
were a considerable number of areas where schools were inaccessible
for many children and often those who did go attended only during the
winter months, at other times they were working to help with the family income. In remote parishes schoolmasters were often poorly paid and
inadequately qualified. Further, it was questionable whether the Church
had the means or the will to do anything about what appeared to be a
deteriorating situation. Where heritors were failing to provide funding
for schools and schoolmasters the Church seems to have found it difficult
to make them. In his submission to the *Statistical Account* the minister
of Morvern in the Presbytery of Argyll complained that although the
schoolmaster's salary had been secured by a decree of the Commissioners
of Supply none of the heritors except the Duke of Argyll had paid their
share and that it would cost too much for the presbytery or the schoolmaster to take them to court. This problem of non-compliance was sometimes exacerbated by the fact that so many of the heritors were absentee
landlords. For example in the parish of Girvan out of ten heritors only
one resided in the parish. Stewart Brown described the situation in Fife
where, as in many other parts of rural Scotland, new farming methods
meant unemployment and poverty for farm laborers but increased wealth
and prosperity for landowners:

> The Fifeshire gentry began emulating the manners and morals of
> their English counterparts. Non-resident landlords became more
> common, as landed families achieved the degree of opulence
> which enabled them to reside most of the year in Edinburgh or

London . . . The children of the gentry were removed from the parish schools, and either educated at home by tutors or sent to public schools in England.[35]

Across the nation the pace of social change was beginning to quicken. Since the 1745 Rebellion the Highlands of Scotland had seen the gradual collapse of the old traditional patterns of community and labor and a continuing process of displacement and resettlement. In many cases this process caused resentment and created barriers between the crofters and the lairds. The 1770s marked the beginning of what has been described as Scotland's first industrial revolution. New agricultural methods and land improvements were changing the face of the countryside as farmers and landholders strove to meet the needs of an ever-growing population and the expanding industrial townships in the Central Belt. The tobacco trade, the linen and paper industries, and coal-mining entered an era of expansion. All this was due to advances in technology—Hargreave's spinning jenny, Watt's steam-engine, Arkwright's water-frame, Crompton's spinning-mule. With industrialization came urbanization and the population of towns such as Glasgow, Edinburgh, Dundee and Aberdeen increased rapidly. Agricultural improvements led to the displacement of former farm-workers and cottars, creating discontent within the rural population. The term "Clearances" usually associated with the Highlands of Scotland can also be applied to what was happening in the Lowlands at this time. In the *Annals of the Parish*, the minister voices his concern that

> The minds of men were excited to new enterprizes; a new genius, as it were, had descended upon the earth, and there was an erect and out-looking spirit abroad that was not to be satisfied with the taciturn regularity of ancient affairs . . . in the midst of all this commercing and manufacturing, I began to discover signs of decay in the wonted simplicity of our country ways.[36]

The feelings of fear and insecurity which accompanied these social changes were heightened by events in France. News of the French Revolution heightened a climate of tension and unrest and Thomas Paine's *The Rights of Man* (1791–1792) was widely read. Throughout the 1790s in the General Assembly and in presbytery minutes expressions of loyalty to the sovereign and support for what was held to be the God-

35. Brown, *Thomas Chalmers and the Godly Commonwealth in Scotland*, 12.

36. Galt, *Annals of the Parish; The Ayrshire Legatees; The Provost*, 99.

given constitution are even more profuse than normal. The Church was anxious to counteract what it regarded as seditious writings which were being circulated among the people. In November 1793 the Rev George Palmer, a Unitarian minister from Dundee, was tried for publishing a seditious hand-bill on *Liberty and the Right of Universal Suffrage*. He was found guilty and deported for seven years. Trees of liberty were planted up and down the country and there was political rioting in Lanark, Perth, Aberdeen, Dundee and Peebles. With horror and alarm the Church of Scotland recognized that even in Scotland there was support for those principles which had produced anarchy and atheism in France and called on members to defend the Constitution of the country against any violent demands for change. Liberty and equality, as demanded by the radicals, were frightening concepts for most ministers.

Another issue contributing to the unrest of these times was the struggle for electoral reform. Inspired by Paine's writings Friends of the People Societies were founded and in association with similar bodies in England called for a more democratic representation of the people in Parliament. Suggestions that this movement in Scotland, influenced by Thomas Muir, was also associated with a strong republican nationalist sentiment have been explored by John D. Brims who concluded that the Scottish Friends of the People sought to democratize the political process within the framework of the British union.[37] Be that as it may, the actions of Muir and people who shared his views added yet another element to the general agitation. In 1792 there were protest meetings in several of the large burghs after the most recent motion for reform had been talked out by the House of Commons.

The demonizing of the French Revolution with its irreligious influence had quite a different effect in some quarters. It stimulated an enthusiasm for mission and evangelism and an increasing number of lay preachers such as James and Robert Haldane, were to be found spreading their message throughout the country.[38] These preachers with their puritanical zeal took advantage of the social discontent and the suspicion of the parish church prevalent among the Highlanders at this time. In October 1796 a meeting of the Gratis Sabbath School Society was held to plan for the opening of Sabbath Evening Schools in Edinburgh and

37. Brims, "The Scottish 'Jacobins,'" 254.
38. See Appendix 1.1.

its neighborhood. Its object was to set up schools where children would be taught the most important doctrines of Scripture, and not the traditions and interpretation of any particular Christian denomination. Those behind this scheme claimed that religious instruction could not be taught as any other subject but only by teachers who were disciples of Christ whose chief qualification was that they were pious young men and devout women. The first Gratis Sabbath School was opened in March 1797. With similar missionary zeal the Society for the Propagation of the Gospel at Home was started by the Relief Church in 1797 and in 1798 the Glasgow Missionary Society was founded. The popularity of these movements may well have been due to the indifference of the Moderate ministers who had distanced themselves from the search for faith and reassurance among their parishioners.

During this last decade of the century the number of dissenting churches increased throughout the country. In the town of Aberdeen, for example, over and above three parish churches there could be found two Episcopal churches, three Secession churches, a Roman Catholic church, a Methodist church, and a Quaker meeting-house. Some of these denominations were starting up their own schools and there was a considerable growth in the number of Sunday schools, adventure schools and private schools described by Charles Camic as a "multiform welter of privately operated establishments principally financed by student payments."[39] (The Barony of Glasgow is reported to have had fifteen private schools and a charity school supported by David Dale who founded his factory village which included a day school at New Lanark in 1786.) In the words of T. M. Devine, "the educational hegemony of the Kirk was breaking down in the eighteenth century with the dynamic growth of private schools and the expansion of the towns where the role of the Church had always been less significant."[40] Changes in rural life led to a more mobile population which posed further problems for school education. Devine has described one case study showing that two-thirds of the families listed for the village of Kippen in Stirlingshire in 1789 were no longer resident there in 1793. Traditionally there had always been some movement of tradesmen seeking work but by the early nineteenth century it was becoming more and more the norm.

39. Camic, *Experience and Enlightenment*, 142.
40. Devine, *The Scottish Nation 1700–2000*, 99.

By the early 1790s these issues forced the Kirk look again at its responsibility for schooling. It had seen its authority questioned. It feared the influence of the French Revolution and the social restlessness and threat to traditional moral values caused by it. It saw how influential evangelical lay preachers like the Haldane brothers had been and the information gathered for the *Statistical Account* by ministers had highlighted the deficiencies of school education throughout the nation. These were factors which all helped rouse the Kirk to action. Certainly it was no coincidence that the two most important pieces of legislation dealing with school education to be passed for several decades were brought forward in the last six years of the eighteenth century.

THE AWAKENING OF THE KIRK

Apart from emphatically expressing loyalty to the King and Constitution, supporting the war effort and denouncing the dangerous principles of the French, the records of the General Assembly in the years immediately prior to 1793 show little awareness of the social changes that were rapidly taking place in the world around it. Certainly there seems to have been little attempt to consider how school education might be developed to meet the needs of the rural and urban developments described above. It continued to rely very much on the Royal Bounty supplementing and supporting the activities of the SSPCK. It was an overture by a Mr. Rankin, a commissioner to the 1794 General Assembly, who had expressed concern at the state of religious education that eventually persuaded the Church to take positive action with regard to schools. In its response to this overture the Assembly decided that the neglect of religious education in schools was largely to blame for the increasing immorality of the times. The result was that the Assembly passed an *Act and Resolution respecting the Religious Education of Youth*. As a means of dealing with what was seen as a growing evil, this Act enjoined all parish schoolmasters and teachers in schools under the superintendence of the Church, to ensure that the Bible was read in schools regularly and that children memorized the Shorter Catechism. Ministers were instructed to visit and examine schools and teachers and presbyteries were instructed to visit schools at least once a year and to report on their diligence to the next Assembly. In 1795 the Assembly appointed a committee to classify these returns (The Committee on the Returns of Presbyteries as to Schools) and again reminded presbyteries to pay particular attention to their responsibilities. Here was the Church's first attempt to enforce a law relating to school inspection. That the Assembly believed it necessary to adopt these measures was an acknowledgement that up until then kirk sessions and presbyteries had been remiss in their superintendence of schools and had failed to identify that religious education had been neglected in schools throughout the country. This Act is notable in that it required the visitation not only of parish schools but also of schools in cities and towns. Whereas in cities such as Dundee and Glasgow committees had already been set up to carry out and report on regular inspections of schools, the wording of most presbytery minutes following the 1794 Act implies that for most of them any kind of systematic or organized visitation of schools was a novel idea. In April 1795 Edinburgh Presbytery agreed that the best way to implement the Act was to create a number of committees to examine schools in different parts of the Presbytery. In less than two months it had visited seventy-eight schools. This included a visit to the High School by representatives of the Presbytery and the magistrates. That year saw other presbyteries adopting the same procedure. Almost all inspections, however, adhered closely to the wording of the Act and reported only on the Bible being read and the Catechism taught. There is no indication of any other subjects being examined. In Dundee and Glasgow where the visitation of schools had been put in place prior to 1794, the reason for their attentiveness may have been that with the rapid expansion of industry and commerce, there was a felt need for ensuring that young people would be better prepared to take up the increasing number of new jobs. In Glasgow, where there were no parish schools, the schoolmasters to be examined would be teachers in private or endowed schools and hospitals. Here again we have another example of a presbytery applying the existing legislation in the case of all schools and not just to parish schools.

It is important to recognize that the 1794 debate centered on "Religious Education." (This is in itself an interesting term as one would have expected *Religious Instruction* which was the term which came to be used and was later enshrined in the preamble to the 1872 Education [Scotland] Act.) At this time the main the concern seems to have been not with education generally but with the morality of the young, reflecting the traditional attitude of the Church that one of the great aims of education should be the godly upbringing of young people for the peace and prosperity of the nation. The 1794 Act does not define the immorality it had in mind—what it described as "the growth in licentiousness"—presumably it included the rise in whisky consumption, illegitimacy rates and Sabbath-breaking. No doubt it also included the republican atheism associated with the French Revolution.

Further social and religious developments towards the end of the eighteenth century convinced the Church that the 1794 Act had not gone far enough as far as the oversight of the nation's moral welfare and the supervision of schools were concerned. The increase in Sunday schools outside the control of the Church of Scotland and the growing strength of the Secession churches began to alarm the Moderate Party which, though no longer as influential, still held sway in the Assembly. Further, concern had been expressed by many synods about the number of unqualified ministers and preachers conducting services. The response of the Assembly when it met in 1799 was first to pass a "Declaratory Act Respecting Unqualified Ministers and Preachers," and then to issue a "Pastoral Admonition by the General Assembly to the People under their Charge." The Act warned ministers not to allow those not ordained or not licensed by the Church of Scotland to use their pulpits. The Admonition, which was to be read in all churches, warned members against false teachers, revolutionary principles and seditious books, pamphlets, and tracts. It specifically pointed out the danger of the Society for the Propagation of the Gospel at Home and the Sunday schools it had established. The Assembly was particularly worried about missionaries from this Society who were going in to parishes, masquerading as teachers, and setting up Sunday schools without the permission of presbyteries, ministers, or heritors. The outcome was the adoption by the Assembly of the *Report Concerning Vagrant Teachers and Sunday Schools*. This was the last major piece of legislation drawn up by the Moderate party. It certainly was an indication of the Church's increasing fears for the future of school education. The action it took was no doubt strengthened by the fact that it was to this General Assembly sitting in 1799 that Sir John Sinclair presented the newly published *Statistical Account of Scotland* with its depressing comments about the state of schools.

With this legislation the Church acted in the belief that the best means of defense was attack. It sought once more to impose its authority by pronouncing as illegal schools set up outside its jurisdiction. The 1799 report began by recapitulating the various Acts from 1565 to the middle of the eighteenth century that laid down the Church's right to superintend all schoolmasters and teachers. It was anxious to remind the nation that its authority in matters of school education and the supervision of schoolmasters had been engrossed in the Treaty of Union. It recalled that the right to examine all teachers and schoolmasters extended not only to those in parish schools but also to teachers in private schools and in schools set up by other denominations. Parents and families were warned against employing tutors and teachers who had not been examined and approved by the presbytery. In conclusion it enjoined all presbyteries to be diligent in exercising those powers which the law of the land had entrusted to them and to ensure all schoolmasters were sufficiently qualified. Presbyteries were instructed to submit to the following Assembly reports detailing lists of schools, the number of pupils attending, the subjects taught, the provisions made for the schoolmaster, and whether the schools were held on Sundays or on other days of the week. That there might be some opposition to the Church enforcing what it regarded as its legal rights, is anticipated by a recommendation that the Procurator of the Church should be ready to give his assistance and, at public expense, take the necessary action to assist the Church in this task.

From the date of this injunction until an Education Committee was proposed in 1824, the General Assembly received reports on matters concerning schools and schoolmasters with increasing frequency but, it has to be said, also with increasing frustration at the continuing lack of diligence on the part of many presbyteries. When the Committee on Vagrant Teachers and Sunday Schools reported to the Assembly of 1800 it had to admit that less than a quarter of the Presbyteries had made any report, and this was to be the pattern year after year thus making it impossible for the Assembly to compose an overall picture of the school situation. To add to the Assembly's difficulties, questions were raised as to the competency and accuracy of presbytery reports. It was claimed that a presbytery, in measuring the success and progress of a school or the efficiency of a schoolmaster, would find it difficult to compare schools given their different circumstances and also the fact that there were no fixed standards of proficiency by which they could be judged. Presbyteries may have been qualified to examine a schoolmaster on his faith and character and even on his academic achievements but not on his ability to teach, which was a different matter altogether. Moreover, until an official format for submitting reports was devised by the Assembly, there was no way of standardizing school visitations, each presbytery being left to carry them out as it saw fit. There is some evidence that from time to time Burgh schools continued to oppose any examination by presbyteries. It took an Assembly judgment in 1817, for example, to assert the Presbytery of Brechin's indisputable right to examine all types of schools within their bounds, in the face of what had been opposition from the Magistrates and Council of the burgh of Montrose. In addition more teachers were refusing to sign the Church's Formula by which they subscribed to the Christian Faith. To try to tighten things up and make the reports from presbyteries more structured and so more comparable, a standardized printed schedule was produced. This listed questions regarding the number of parish schools established and needed in each parish, the salary and accommodation provided for the schoolmaster, and what other kinds of schools were in operation. In 1820 copies of this schedule were sent to every parish minister, to be completed and returned to the presbytery but when only a third of presbyteries showed any willingness to cooperate by using the new forms it was obvious that the Church was powerless to enforce its own regulations and that some other means of supervising schools and establishing the Church's authority in education would need to be found.

A number of other factors highlighted the need for urgent action. There was in some quarters opposition to the whole idea of a better universal education. Following the mass demonstrations of the "Radical War" in Scotland and the Peterloo massacre in England, both in support of parliamentary reform, it appears that there were some who saw unrest among the working classes as arising from improvements in their schooling. There was a danger in ordinary people becoming too articulate. Further where reports identified places where schools were needed, for example in the expanding industrial towns of Paisley, Greenock, Port Glasgow and Renfrew where there were no parish schools, the Church had no means of establishing new schools or appointing teachers. In addition any control which the Church had over school education was weakened by the growing number of dissenter schools and private schools and Catholic schools where teachers believed themselves to be outside the Church of Scotland's jurisdiction.[41] Within the Church itself missionary and evangelical pres-

---

41. The Catholic Schools Society was founded in Glasgow in 1817. It was established by a group of merchants and was managed by a committee, half of whom were Catholics and half Protestants. They appointed Catholic teachers who used a Protestant version of the Bible.

sure was being brought to bear on the Moderate party of the Church by the Evangelical Party which was growing in power and popularity and was encouraging in some quarters a more parish-orientated ministry. One result of this was an increase in the number of Sessional schools[42] established and managed by congregations and so not directly under the control of the General Assembly. The inspiration behind this new movement was undoubtedly Thomas Chalmers who instituted the first parish Sabbath-school society in Glasgow in 1816 and opened the first parish school there in 1820.

In the years preceding the General Assembly's decision in 1824 to look into the possibility of setting up a committee with the specific remit of establishing schools where the management and curriculum would be under its direct control, these factors helped to persuade parish ministers that it was time for the Church to act. In the end the General Assembly was convinced of the necessity for immediate action by the results of Brougham's survey. Co-incidentally, and perhaps intentionally satirically, the edition of the *Scotsman* newspaper which reported on the Presbytery's discussion of Baird's motion, also carried a leader which commented: "We are glad to see that the state of education in *Edinburgh* is to be inquired into. At a recent meeting of Presbytery, Dr. A. Thomson remarked humorously on the disobedience in this respect of the clergy of Edinburgh, to the injunctions of the General Assembly. There certainly has been a supineness here; but the clergy, we trust, will now work along with the laity, not merely in promoting education, but in ascertaining the circumstances and improving the condition of the poor. The mechanism of the established church may be useful here."[43]

It now remained to be seen whether a "supine" clergy who had in the past often been neglectful of their duties towards schools, would be more supportive of the new initiative which was being proposed.

42. Schools set up and funded by Kirk Sessions.
43. *Scotsman*, 3 April 1824.

Appendix 1.1

The setting up of independent Sunday schools in many of the principal towns in Scotland and the founding of the Society for the Propagation of the Gospel at Home were largely the work of James Haldane. These Sunday schools were mainly evangelical in purpose and should not be confused with the "Sunday schools" (schools held on Sundays) which had already been set up in a number of places to provide education for children who could not attend weekday schools either because they were working or because their parents could not afford the fees. These schools also helped to take wilder youngsters off the streets on the Sabbath. The minutes of the Presbytery of Langholm for September 1799 record the Presbytery considering setting up Sunday schools "in the light of the progressive improvement of manufacturers and of advancing population." The Statistical Account for the City of Glasgow states that eleven Sunday schools were begun in 1787. In the wake of the French revolution the spread of Sunday schools associated with Haldane and lay preachers at this time led many in the Church of Scotland to regard the whole Sunday School movement with suspicion.

2

The First Ten Years

*It is impossible to resist the conclusion that our ancient system of popu-
lar instruction is in an alarming condition and that, if we really wish to
make our parish schools continue to accomplish the purposes for which
they were originally designed, we must cease to slumber over them with
the half patriarchal half poetical dream which is apt to come over us
when we think of those rural seminaries . . . and must do something
effectual to revive them.*

—Henry Cockburn, 1827

A COMMITTEE IS SET UP

IN 1824, AWARE OF the inability of the existing scheme to meet the
educational needs of the country and inspired by a desire to keep faith
with the ideals of the Reformers, the General Assembly of the Church of
Scotland took the bold step of contemplating the provision of an educational system of its own. In doing so it was no doubt encouraged by those
parish churches which had already successfully established Sessional
schools. While the Church pursued this course of action out of a genuine
aspiration to meet people's educational needs and to provide a system
which would encourage social mobility and self-improvement, there
were other motives at work. In the years that followed it emerged that the
Church was driven also by the desire to safeguard religious instruction
and to exercise its moral and social control of the nation which it saw
threatened by the rise in the number of adventure schools and schools associated with dissenting churches and by those instances where its super-

intendence of schools was questioned.[1] C. G. Brown has calculated that by 1826, 38 percent of the Scottish people were dissenters.[2] In March 1824 Edinburgh Presbytery agreed to transmit to the forthcoming General Assembly an overture drawn up by Principal George Baird calling on the Assembly to appoint a committee to produce a plan for "increasing the means of education and of religious instruction throughout Scotland in general, where this may be needful, particularly in the Highlands and Islands, and in large and populous cities, where, in these times, the children of the poor demand the most deliberate and careful attention."[3]

Baird claimed that in spite of the fact that landed proprietors were attending to the erection of schools as far as could reasonably be expected the number of children not attending any school was greater than what was generally believed. Figures in Brougham's report had indicated that schools continued to be very scarce in the Synods of Argyll, Glenelg, Sutherland and Caithness and Baird urged support for his overture from ministers and elders as the official guardians of the intellectual as well as the moral and religious welfare of the people of Scotland. The Assembly unanimously accepted the terms of Baird's overture and agreed to appoint a committee with him as convener to make inquiries and collate the relevant facts and to come back to the next Assembly with a plan which the Church might adopt. The Assembly further instructed its committee to find out what help heritors might be willing to offer and what funding, if any, the Government might provide for any proposed scheme.

And so it was that in 1825 the General Assembly of the Church of Scotland confirmed the appointment of an Education Committee (*The Committee on increasing the means of Education and Religious Instruction in Scotland and in particular in the Highlands and Islands*), with the aim of extending and improving school education in Scotland.[4] In the fulfilment of this aim the committee set itself to address four issues: the need for

1. Sir John Sinclair estimated that, according to the returns in the Parliamentary Report of 1818, out of 5,081 elementary schools, 2,479 were fee-paying private schools (*Analysis of the Statistical Account of Scotland*, Part II 98–99).

2. Brown, "Religion and Social Change," 151.

3. Baird, *Extracts from reports of the ministers of parishes in some synods of Scotland: made in 1818 and 1819, as to parochial schools*, iii, and see the *Scotsman*, 3 April 1824 for a similar wording of the Overture and extracts from the ensuing debate.

4. At the previous General Assembly in May 1824, a committee had been set up to look into the case for establishing an Education Committee. This may be taken as the start of the new committee.

more schools; the need to train schoolmasters and improve their conditions of service; the need to promote and develop the regular examination of schools by presbyteries and parish ministers; and the need to safeguard the place of religious instruction, or perhaps more accurately, instruction in Protestant doctrines, in the school curriculum. To begin the process it was agreed to raise funds by appealing to the generosity of the nation through Church collections. Once sufficient funds had been raised schoolmasters or catechists were to be appointed in areas that appeared most needful after the heritors and others concerned had been informed.

Since, by 1824, the Brougham report was some six years old, the Education Committee decided, that in determining the priority of locations for the first Church schools, it first had to obtain up-to-date information on the existing educational provision. Accordingly a list of questions was sent out to parish ministers. Out of the 907 ministers approached some eight hundred sent in returns, a proportion which indicated a considerable interest in the project. The new data confirmed Brougham's findings that the six northernmost Synods with 143 parishes had the most immediate need. It was estimated that at least 10,500 children in these Synods were without the means of education and that not less than 250 additional schools and 130 catechists were required. In one parish of 1,000 square miles and a population of 4,747, only 995 had learned to read. Gaelic, being mainly a spoken language in the Highlands, presented the challenge of teaching people to read in Gaelic as well as in English. Few schoolmasters were sufficiently fluent in both languages and the geography of these areas made it difficult for children to attend school. The information gleaned from the returns also showed that the rest of Scotland with 764 parishes in the Lowlands, the Central belt and the East, was well supplied with the means of education, and that there was scarcely an individual who had not been taught to read. Probably these figures only reflected the views of ministers in the existing rural parishes and took little account of the situation in the new urban developments. Both Thomas Chalmers and David Stow were very much aware of the acute shortage of schools in the expanding industrial areas. Indeed, describing the efforts of Chalmers and Stow to set up first Sunday schools and then day schools in Glasgow, the Scottish historian Stewart Mechie has commented that as soon as Stow came out into the open with his views and suggestions he was confronted with all the self-satisfaction of the Scottish educational tradition and the complacency of those who did not realize the evils to be remedied.[5]

THE FIRST ASSEMBLY SCHOOLS

In June 1825 the main Education Committee, comprising over forty members, appointed an Acting Sub-Committee of eight (four ministers and four elders) as an administrative executive to make day-to-day decisions and produce reports which then went to the main committee. George Baird acted as Convener and John Gordon as Secretary of this sub-committee which, with men like Dr. Andrew Thomson and Dr. John Lee as members, represented both the Moderate and Evangelical parties.[6]

Raising enough money to start the work was obviously the primary concern. Baird had informed the Assembly that in carrying out their remit they had the backing of the heritors in the Highlands and Islands who were prepared to give the Church's efforts every support. In a pamphlet published in 1819 Thomas Chalmers had examined alternative means of funding school education and had reached the conclusion that he favored a system where education was partly endowed and partly paid for from fees. It was this system that the committee also decided to adopt and incorporate into its *Regulations* to be followed by teachers in conducting their Schools. As a first step towards raising the necessary funding the committee sent out leaflets describing the deplorable want of schools in the Highlands and Islands. Several copies went to every minister for distribution in his parish with a reminder that collections should be made and annual subscriptions encouraged in aid of the committee's work. As a result of this appeal 420 parishes sent up contributions which, together with other donations and subscriptions, raised a total income for the committee of £5,488. This was a commendable amount for a first effort given that there were already many benevolent charities appealing for support.

Next the committee had to put its mind to deciding where and how to begin spending this money. It reached the decision that in the first

---

5. Mechie, *The Church and Scottish Social Development*, 142. The Glasgow Infant School Society was formed in 1826 with Stow as secretary. For further information on Chalmers and Stow see Appendix 1.

6. Andrew Thomson had set up a school in Young Street in Edinburgh in 1824. In 1834 this school had a master, an assistant, and seven monitors; the master was paid £84 a year, the assistant £32, and the monitors "according to efficiency" (Law, *Edinburgh Schools of the Nineteenth Century*, 14).

instance it would limit itself to locating places before interviewing and appointing teachers so yet another questionnaire was dispatched this time to more than two hundred ministers throughout the country who had made special requests for schools in their returns to the 1824 inquiry. Instead of confining this latest survey to ministers in the Highlands and Islands the committee made a point of sending it out to every parish in Scotland where requests for schools had been made in order to identify those places of greatest need. At the same time local landowners in these parishes were kept informed in the hope that they might offer possible accommodation for schools. This step seems to have paid off for in November 1825 the committee was able to take up an offer of a site provided by the Society for British Fisheries and open its first school at Ullapool. So active and diligent was the committee in pursuing its ends that by the time the General Assembly met in 1826 it was able to report on forty-one locations where schools had been opened or where there were plans for building.

Recognizing that school education in Scotland at this time presented a bewildering scene with wide variations in what pupils might be offered and how schools might be managed, it was important that early on the committee should set out guidelines and regulations with regard to where schools were to be sited and how they were to be run.[7] Right from the outset the committee made it clear that in its choice of location it would adopt the same principle as the SSPCK had embraced some eighty years earlier, namely that it had no intention of relieving heritors of their statutory duties and would therefore not set up a new school in any parish where there was not already a parish school. At the same time any new school would be located far enough away from the parish school so as not to be in competition with it. There would need to be a sufficient number of school-age children to justify the new school building and to provide the necessary income from fees for the schoolmaster. In spite of low salaries and poor conditions, there was no shortage of applicants for schoolmasters' posts. In the nine months following the first advertisement one hundred and thirty applications were received. Applicants were interviewed and had to produce certification of their moral character and religious affiliation, their teaching experience, and their ability.

---

7. These are reproduced in full at the end of this chapter as Appendix 2.2.

The Education Committee faced the difficulty of employing school-masters at a time when, as we have seen, there was considerable discontent in that profession. The morale of teachers was low. Among them there were always some who had failed to obtain their qualifications in divinity and who taught in the schools as "stickit ministers." In sparsely populated areas of the Highlands and in cities like Glasgow many school-masters could only afford to teach part-time and had to earn a living by taking on other jobs. In an article in the *Edinburgh Review* in 1827, Henry Cockburn, discussing the impoverished state of schoolmasters, pointed out that the arrangements for "side schools" provided for by the 1803 Act had actually made matters worse since the salary had to be divided between the two masters and there was no house provided for the second teacher. What today we might describe as a parish schoolmasters' "take-home pay" (or total emoluments) is notoriously difficult to calculate since it included what the heritors paid as a salary together with what he received by way of fees and earnings from other sources such as acting as Session Clerk or as Precentor at Sunday services or for administering the poor fund. Heritors were also required to supply the schoolhouse, a dwelling-house of at least two apartments, a small garden, free fuel, and a piece of land for keeping a cow during the summer and winter and, when the latter two could not be obtained, a sufficient compensation in lieu of them. The amount earned from fees varied from school to school depending on its locality, the number of pupils, and the number of subjects offered. Norman MacLeod, a famous nineteenth century Glasgow minister, has given us an account of the situation from his personal experience: "His emoluments for all this labor were not extravagant. Let us calculate. He had £15 as schoolmaster; £5 in school fees; £7 as postmaster; £1 as session clerk; £1 as leader of church psalmody; £5 as catechist: £34 in all, with house and garden."[8]

The basic salary paid by the Education Committee was £20–£25 per annum which was about the minimum paid to parish schoolmasters by the heritors at that time. It also compared fairly well with that paid by other charitable organizations. Assembly schoolmasters were disadvantaged, however, in that they were not eligible for many of the extra perquisites enjoyed by the parish schoolmaster.

8. MacLeod *Reminiscences of a Highland Parish,* 215. While minister in the Barony Church Glasgow MacLeod helped to provide school accommodation for two thousand children.

In 1828 the "Report of the Committee on the Returns as to Schools," drew attention to the provision made in the 1803 Act that there should be a revision of the parish schoolmasters' salaries every twenty-five years and so that year salaries were raised from £16 to £25 for those on the minimum salary and from £22 to £34 for those on the maximum. Taking the average salary as about £30 and adding £25 for school fees gave the schoolmaster approximately £55 per annum. Six years later a committee of Scottish schoolmasters asked the Assembly to support its petition to the government for salaries to be raised by one chalder. It was claimed that an additional chalder worth about £17 at that time would raise the average salary to £72.[9] Other requests were that the school houses which were provided should have more rooms and that the required qualification for schoolmasters should include a competent knowledge of Latin and Greek. The question of salaries and housing, however, was only part of a wider discussion which included the whole method of appointing and supervising schoolmasters and there were those who thought this should be looked at before any salary rise was awarded. There were complaints that parish schoolmasters were negligent in the discharge of their duties and it was suggested that there should be a radical reform of the method of appointing and removing them. One proposal was that heads of families in each parish should choose them instead of leaving it to the heritors and the presbytery, and that they should be on a six or seven year contract. The public debate was kept alive by a motion in the House of Commons in June 1834 by J. C. Colquhoun, MP for Dunbartonshire, presenting a bill to regulate and enlarge the provision for parish education in Scotland.

Concurrently with this debate about the competency of schoolmasters and how they should be appointed and supervised, a committee of the Presbytery of Glasgow produced a long and detailed report which contained a number of important recommendations with regard to the presbytery's supervision of schools. This report is important in that it not only stressed the importance of each minister reporting annually on all schools in his parish, it also emphasized the need to ensure that teachers who were interviewed not only had the necessary academic qualifications, but knew how to communicate with young people. The importance of encouraging the community as well as the heritors to take an active

9. The *chalder* was a measure of oatmeal or grain the value of which varied according to agreed market prices, which could differ from district to district and year to year.

interest in their parish schools was noted as well as the requirement that each school day should open with prayer and that religious instruction should be given its proper place with the Bible being read to the class daily by the teacher. This was a remarkable attempt not only to achieve a thorough implementation of the existing system of school examination, but also to ensure that teaching skills were included in any inspection.

In spite of the uncertainties and hardships experienced by the teaching profession, the Church's Education Committee had no difficulties recruiting schoolmasters with the necessary dedication and qualifications for its new schools. By 1834 it had made 139 appointments and established some eighty-six schools providing an education for 6,610 scholars in some of the remotest areas of the Highlands. From the moderate amount of funding raised from congregations, however, it was clear that the scheme still did not have the whole hearted support of the Church. Perhaps this was due to the many other commitments of Church members but it is also possible that some in Lowland Scotland still bore a grudge against the Highlanders whom they associated with Jacobite and Episcopalian sympathies.

SCHOOL INSPECTION AND PRESBYTERY RETURNS

To help them decide where to locate schools Baird and his committee also had access to the annual statistics collated by the Assembly "Committee on the Returns of Presbyteries as to Schools." These were of some assistance in identifying areas of greatest need. However, as before, the value of these returns was diminished by the diffident and off-hand way presbyteries dealt with them. While some made use of the regular printed forms others continued to devise their own ways of tabulating their findings and some only sent in scribbled notes. Many of the returns were incomplete and details were missing. So many irregular and scanty returns meant that it was impossible for the Education Committee to construct a full picture of the school situation throughout the land. Nevertheless the information supplied was generally comparable, listing all the schools in a parish, the type of school (e.g., parish, burgh, private, SSPCK), the number of scholars attending, the subjects taught, the religious affiliation and qualification of the schoolmaster, and some brief remarks supplied by those who had visited the school. For example the Presbytery of Abernethy noted that the drop in numbers attending schools was due to the uncommonly bad rainy season which held up the cutting of the peats for fuel. In many cases the remarks noted that religious instruction was being given and added a comment on the general standard of education. Presbyteries were always looking for teachers with good academic qualifications who could offer a broad curriculum even in fairly small schools. The Church's insistence that its schedules should be completed by presbyteries at least kept the Church's right to visit and inspect schools in the public eye at a time when some would have liked to see the Established Church's statutory powers diminished and at a time when, distracted by other controversial issues such as Patronage, education was not as high on the Church's agenda as the Education Committee might have hoped. Of course there were times when individual teachers made things difficult for a presbytery. Two teachers in Meigle categorically refused to meet with the presbytery declaring that they did not consider themselves subject to its jurisdiction either as individuals or as teachers. Somewhat in the Highland tradition of "The Men," there were schoolmasters who fancied themselves as preachers and who took to exhorting the people and refused to attend public worship as would normally have been expected of schoolmasters.[10] Some of these teachers regarded school education as only a secondary concern, preaching being their main interest.

One of the most remarkable facts noted in the Presbyterial Returns was the number and variety of private schools throughout the country. As the demand for education had increased and the existing parish and burgh schools had proved insufficient, private enterprise had filled the gaps. It has been estimated that by the end of the Napoleonic Wars twice as many children in Scotland were receiving some kind of education in private schools as in the parish schools and that by 1850, some thirty-five years later, there were at least nine or ten types of schools in Scotland.[11] The extensive variety of small private schools, often existing in close proximity, is seen in the way they were designated in the returns by street names or by the name of the schoolmaster. The High Church Parish in

10. Going back as early as the middle of the eighteenth century and lasting as influential up to the time of the Disruption, "The Men" were formidable charismatic lay preachers, often better-off crofters or tradesmen, with an intense spiritual commitment and a commanding knowledge of Scripture, who exercised considerable power and influence over the people in the central and southern Highlands, often regarding the Moderates in the parish ministry as ungodly.

11. Mechie, *The Church and Scottish Social Development*, 138 and 147.

Edinburgh, for example, listed three private day schools in Carrubber's Close, an SSPCK school in Warriston's Close, and a school in Anchor Close established and supported by a Mrs. Douglas of Cavers. There was a school in the Castle established by the Government for children with army connections and at Cramond there was a Female School supported by Lady Rosebery chiefly for children on Lord Rosebery's estate.

The statistics also revealed a wide diversity of provision both in the curriculum offered and in the qualifications of the teachers who delivered it. Almost half of the schoolmasters in parish schools had completed a four-year university course. In the towns the parish and burgh schools offered a fairly comprehensive curriculum often including Latin and sometimes Greek and French. Ayr Academy curriculum, for example, covered Mathematics, Natural Philosophy, Chemistry, Geography, Languages Ancient and Modern, Writing, Drawing, and English Grammar and Composition. It would appear, however, that in the parish schools in the rural areas and in private schools in particular, the curriculum was usually very basic, covering little more than reading, writing and counting. There were, however, a number of fascinating exceptions. In the small parish school at Lochalsh with 98 pupils, Greek and Latin were taught, and in a private school in Keith an Episcopalian minister taught French and Hebrew. In the parish school attended by some fifty children in the small town of Lochmaben (population c.2,000) in the south-west of Scotland subjects taught included English, Latin, Greek, French, writing, arithmetic, navigation, mathematics, and geography. For its part the Church attempted to offer an equally wide curriculum in its schools even in rural areas. In the small Assembly school at Barvas in the Presbytery of Lewis, the scholars were taught Gaelic, English, writing, arithmetic, mathematics, Latin, and Greek, while in Dunoon the Assembly school is recorded as teaching, English, Latin, Greek, French, Gaelic, writing, arithmetic, navigation, book-keeping, and geography. Even where this range of subjects was offered, however, it is not clear is how many pupils actually took advantage of the whole curriculum. For example, from the Education Committee Report to the General Assembly in 1834 it appears that Latin was taught at 29 out of the 86 Assembly schools, but only to 89 pupils.

The records show that in most parish schools the schoolmasters were members of the Established Church and were "qualified to Government," that is, they had signed the Church's Confession of Faith (the "Formula") and taken the oath of allegiance to the Government. In most private schools, on the other hand, the returns show that teachers were not qualified in this way and belonged to a variety of religious persuasions. The return of the Presbytery of Edinburgh in 1830 described teachers in private and society schools in the parish of North Leith as belonging to the Established Church, the Secession Church, the Auld Licht Antiburghers, the Roman Catholic Church, and the Baptist Church. In some cases teachers were Church of Scotland probationers. Strangely enough when the Education Committee was employing teachers in its own schools it would appear that it did not always make being "qualified to government" a condition of employment.

The decision of the Assembly in 1824 was the first time the Church of Scotland had actually taken steps to establish its own schools and it is important to consider the Church's motives and aims in pursuing such an undertaking. If, as has been suggested, the committee was inspired by the inspiration and example of Knox and the First Book of Discipline then it is difficult to avoid the conclusion that much of the work was motivated by the desire to give people a basic education so that they would be equipped to read and in particular to read the Bible. Time and again when the Education Committee reviewed its progress, its great regret was always the number who were still unable to read. Further from the outset the remit given to the committee was to increase the means of education *and* Religious Instruction throughout Scotland. Any inspection of schools had to be conducted bearing in mind the philosophy, or maybe rather the theology, that lay behind the Church's involvement with education. Presbyteries were specifically asked to report on the quality of the religious instruction being given in all schools, including the use of the Church Catechism and the Scriptures. Reporting in 1832 the Education Committee felt able to claim that, thanks to the superintendence of presbyteries and the testing of teachers' religious knowledge on appointment, religious instruction was the best taught subject in most schools. The Church insisted that in its own schools the school day should be opened and closed with prayer and the Scriptures should be read daily as a school book. The Mother's Catechism[12] and the Shorter Catechism were to be taught and school books compiled by Andrew Thomson were to be used

12. This was a catechism produced to explain the meaning of the Shorter Catechism. It was the work of the Reverend John Willison (1680–1750) and published in Edinburgh in 1731.

for teaching Psalms, Paraphrases, and passages of Scripture. The Church also placed importance on Sunday schools (at that time often described as "Sabbath" schools) which it regarded as an extension or continuation of weekday schools particularly as they offered opportunities for religious instruction to those in Highland areas who lived far from any place of public worship.

It would be wrong, however, to conclude from such statements that the advancement of religious belief or the desire to recruit church members were the only aims, or even the primary aims, of the committee. There was a hunger for education generally and the Education Committee's efforts were always directed at satisfying that hunger by providing a secular education comparable with what was available in other schools. This approach is highlighted by the emphasis put on the qualifications and training it demanded. In 1828 the convener and secretary of the committee completed a tour of inspection of Assembly schools and noted that two types of schools were emerging corresponding to the ability of the schoolmasters and the districts in which they were situated. The aim in all schools was to teach the majority of pupils to read (mainly in English but also in Gaelic where appropriate), to write and to count, but in the higher or more advanced category of Assembly schools able and interested pupils were given the opportunity to study subjects such as geography, mathematics, astronomy and languages such as French, Greek and Latin, a curriculum which compared favorable with what was offered in many burgh schools. As always, however, a true picture of the situation has to take into account the number of pupils actually taking some of these subjects. Out of 5,670 pupils attending Assembly schools at that time only 63 took Latin, 21 took practical mathematics (mensuration) and 16 geography. This would remain more or less the pattern over the next six years although numbers taking any one subject (apart from English and Gaelic) fluctuated so much from year to year that trends are difficult to identify and, as with parish schools, there were always a few doing some subject out of the ordinary.

Since, at least to begin with, most schools were in the Highlands and Islands, the committee had to decide how much teaching was to be in Gaelic and how much in English. As a working compromise the committee printed sets of school-books in both languages but noted that it expected the English language to be taught in nearly all schools. School-books had to be bought by the scholars and, to encourage reading plans were made to organize itinerating libraries in some places. When the convener and secretary inspected schools they paid particular attention to the needs of the Gaelic population and to the appropriateness of the education provided for females. Education to be provided for girls was to be "suited to the stations in life for which they were destined!" For this purpose the committee proposed to build-on suitable premises to existing schools. It was felt that the personal interest demonstrated by such visits was a way of encouraging and checking up on teachers as well as convincing the heritors that the scheme was being well managed and worth supporting. The possibility of appointing a full-time inspector of schools was explored in 1829 but it was agreed that in the meantime this job was best left to the convener and to deputations from the committee—so much for relying on presbytery supervision and reporting!

Perhaps the curriculum adopted by the Education Committee reflected the two traditional strands which ran through Scottish education. On the one hand there were those who saw the purpose of education as not only providing a "godly upbringing," but also as equipping young people to earn a livelihood and so be an asset to the nation. Here the emphasis was on the academic as much as on the spiritual. In the words of the First Book of Discipline beyond the elementary stage young people, "if they be found apt to learning and letters . . . they must be charged to continue their studie, so that the Commonwealth may have some comfort by them."[13] On the other hand there were many who were inclined to regard education more as a tool to influence and shape the moral and social behavior of the nation and believed that that more importance should be placed on the character and Christian beliefs of the schoolmasters.

By the mid-1830s there were a number of influential voices, like that of George Lewis, who, in his pamphlet *Scotland a Half-Educated Nation, both in the Quantity and Quality of her Education Institutions* sought to draw attention to the importance of concepts such as patriotism and piety and who believed that knowledge and righteousness went hand in hand.[14] "If the nation will not pay for the schoolmaster to prevent crime," wrote Lewis, "it must pay tenfold for the repression of social disorder and for coercing an unhappy, dissolute and reckless population." The Reverend

13. Cameron, *The First Book of Discipline*, 132.

14. The pamphlet, *Scotland a Half-Educated Nation*, was published in 1834 and was based on the proceedings of a meeting of the Glasgow Educational Association where papers had been presented on the "Extension of the Parochial Schools of Scotland."

George Lewis had been licensed by the Presbytery of Glasgow in 1828 and was an influential figure. He was editor of the Scottish Guardian newspaper and, with David Stow, was the joint secretary of the Glasgow Educational Society which was founded in 1834 by J. C. Colquhoun, MP, with the aim of establishing a seminary for the training of teachers. Although Lewis would join the Free Church at the Disruption at this time he was a staunch supporter of the Established Church and its connection with parish schools.

Describing a similar point of view the Church historian Stewart Mechie concluded: "Fear of revolutionary outbreaks like the French Revolution was widespread till the middle of the nineteenth century, and it was commonly held that the great antidote was a Bible education. Thus, the aim of education, as far as the town masses at any rate were concerned, was rather moral discipline than the mere training of the mind. Education must involve the production of a good citizen and the only education capable of doing that was an education in which the Bible predominated."[15]

On the whole it would appear that in its schools the Assembly attempted to achieve a balance between these two strands. The Church was anxious to provide a secular education which would prepare young people for life and equip them with the necessary skills. Its aim was to improve the standards and the scope of school education *per se*, as much as to improve the moral conduct of the population.

CURRENT SOCIAL AND RELIGIOUS ISSUES

Financial Demands on Congregations

When, in 1824, Baird requested Edinburgh Presbytery to transmit his overture with approval, he was fully aware that some of its members had other priorities in mind. In his speech he conceded that while he believed that the Church's first duty was to teach the people of Scotland to read and to understand the Gospel, there were others who saw foreign mission as a priority. While the terms of Baird's overture had eventually been approved by the Presbytery of Edinburgh, during the actual debate members of both the Moderate and Evangelical wings of the Church tried to undermine his argument. The Evangelical churchman Andrew

---

15. Mechie, *The Church and Scottish Social Development*, 145.

Thomson declared that while he was fully aware of the seriousness of the situation, he thought the facts were being overstated and he pointed to all that had been achieved by the Scottish Society for Propagating Christian Knowledge and by the Gaelic Society, in establishing schools. In the same vein John Inglis, who sided with the views of the Moderate party, questioned the wisdom of making yet another appeal to the Church for money and reminded the presbytery that there already was an Assembly committee looking at the state of religion in the cities and towns which had recommended that a school supported by Government grants should be established in every parish. While it is true that there was general support for Baird's overture the comments of Inglis and Thomson should not be overlooked. They represented a hesitancy which would manifest itself over the next few years in the failure of the Church at large to provide the substantial funding needed for such an enterprise. In spite of regular appeals to the generosity of congregations, by 1832 the committee's funds showed a deficit of over £500 and regret was expressed then that there could be no further extension of the work until matters improved. That same year the committee reported that throughout the country 224 parishes had never made any contribution by special collections and that less than one fifth of the parishes in Scotland had contributed more than once over the seven years since the work had started. Perhaps, as Inglis indicated, there was a general feeling that, despite the statistics which Baird had produced, existing legislation for setting up schools was adequate and it was up to the heritors to carry out what the law required of them. What appeared to be disinterest when it came to visiting and examining schools, may have been an indication of a resigned acceptance that there was not a lot the Church could do to improve matters given the statutory power and responsibilities of the heritors and the government.

As far as the members of congregations were concerned, the poor support may have been due not to a lack of interest in schools but rather to the fact that there were so many other appeals being made for new and ongoing charitable work. The minutes of the Presbytery of Glasgow show that congregations within the bounds could be expected to contribute, often annually, to a number of good causes, including promoting education and religious instruction in the East Indies, the Glasgow Missionary Society, the Royal Infirmary, the Glasgow Bible Society, the British and Foreign Bible Society, the Glasgow Society for Promoting the Religious Interests of Scottish Settlers in British North America, and even such local one-off appeals as a collection for distressed weavers in Rutherglen. On the same day as the Education Committee had been appointed, the Assembly had also appointed a committee to consider ways of propagating the Gospel in India. It is rather ironic that the man who was reluctant to ask the Church for money for education, John Inglis, was the person who put forward this proposal in the Assembly. Later he would become the first convener of the committee responsible for the management of the mission to India. From the start the Assembly was aware that there might be a clash of interests and it was difficult for congregations and presbyteries to prioritize. As a way of dealing with the problem several presbyteries formed associations to promote the work of the church at home and abroad and to help raise the necessary funds.

Another call on a congregation's charity was the development of what would nowadays be thought of as "Home Mission" or "National Mission" work, much of it inspired by Thomas Chalmers' efforts to revive the parish ministry. Evidence of this new interest was the founding of the Glasgow City Mission in 1826 and the Edinburgh City Mission in 1832. Moreover it has to be remembered that the running costs of churches built to cope with the needs of the growing city parishes and of new churches in the Highlands and Islands fell outwith the responsibility of the heritors and had to be met very largely from local collections. In 1824 Parliament approved a grant of £50,000 for building churches in the Highlands and Islands, and by 1834, forty-three "government churches" had been built in these regions. Between 1790 and 1834 sixty-six chapels had been erected by private contributions.[16] Church extension was a costly business.

Even more likely to affect collections for the work of the Education Committee was the fact that there was a variety of charities involved in school education of one kind or another all appealing to church members for subscriptions. An established society like the Edinburgh Gratis School Society, which set up Sabbath schools, depended on the financial gifts of its friends and supporters, as did the lesser known Edinburgh Society for Promoting the Education for the Poor in Ireland. The SSPCK, which had pioneered the building of charity schools and was probably the largest provider was now finding itself in financial difficulties and had started to cut back on its work. There was also further public and private investment in schools. Morningside School in Edinburgh (which still

16. See Brown, *Thomas Chalmers*, 212–13.

exists in Morningside Road and is now used as an Evangelical Church) was founded in 1823 by four local landowners who sold subscription shares of £10 to prominent people in the district. In his *Memorials* Henry Cockburn described how he had initiated the fund-raising for the Edinburgh Academy: "the sum of £10,000 was subscribed immediately; and afterwards about £2,000 more. We were fiercely opposed by the Town-Council, as we expected . . . but after due discussion and plotting, our contributors finally resolved to proceed." The Academy was opened on 1 October 1824. In 1831 the trustees of Dr Andrew Bell gifted £10,000 for the endowment of a school in Leith.[17] It is evident, therefore, that with all these financial requests being made to church members and the public, the Education Committee was facing an uphill task in attempting to raise funds for the setting up its new schools and perhaps the romantic appeal of missionary work, whether at home or abroad, was likely to have been stronger than that of education.

Social and Political Issues

The Education Committee's endeavors have also to be understood in the context of a climate of unrest and social change of which the Chartist movement and the demand for parliamentary reform were indicative. Many of the problems for the committee, and for the Church as a whole, stemmed from the rapidly growing population and its re-distribution. The population of Scotland increased by 88 percent between the 1750s and 1831. Smout calculated that the rate of growth between 1811 and 1821 had never been equaled in Scottish history and that by 1820 almost half the Scots occupied the central belt where only 37 percent had lived before. For the Church the growth of the new industrial towns posed a number of challenges. There was, for example, the pressing matter of church accommodation. In April 1824 the Presbytery of Glasgow calculated that while in Glasgow there ought to be church accommodation for 61,000, the actual accommodation, including chapels of ease about to be built, was only 27,000. New churches had to be built and new parishes created and endowed. The General Assembly's response to this problem was

17. Andrew Bell (1753–1832) was a Scottish Anglican priest and educationalist and the founder of Madras College, a secondary school in St. Andrews. He pioneered a monitorial system of mutual instruction (the Madras System of Education) whereby children taught one another, the brighter ones teaching the rest.

to appoint an Accommodation Committee in 1828 to seek Government financial support for this church extension.

For the Education Committee the shifting and growing population was a reminder that its remit was to increase the means of education not only in the Highlands and Islands but also in the large cities and towns. There the number on low wages or unemployed meant that there was little hope of families being able to afford private education for their children. This state of affairs was clearly illustrated by J. C. Colquhoun, MP, in a speech to the House of Commons in 1834 when, referring to school education throughout the whole of Scotland and in particular in the towns, he calculated that in Glasgow out of its estimated school-age population only one fourteenth actually attended a school. He pointed out how badly the situation had deteriorated over the preceding thirty years in a town such as Paisley where only one twentieth of school-age children went to school. He recalled that thirty years earlier there had not been a family in Paisley who could not read the Bible whereas now there were on average 3,000 families whose children were growing up wholly untaught. George Lewis argued that the country's former eminence in learning was being destroyed by urban growth, irreligion, and Irish immigration. Social deprivation in the expanding industrial towns raised the question of how the needs of the poor could be met. Within the Church there was an upsurge of evangelicalism which regarded education as an important tool in combating some of the social and moral evils of the time. There had been a dramatic increase in alcoholism and the temperance movement saw drink as a fundamental cause of crime and degradation. Men like Chalmers and Stow believed that in the struggle with poverty, schools run by Christian schoolmasters were the answer and that the government should help to provide these. David Stow and those who helped him establish the Glasgow Infant School Society and later the Glasgow Educational Society emphasized the importance of the system of parish schools to inculcate in young people the doctrines of the Christian faith.

Another major issue in the early 1830s was the agitation for electoral reform. The Radical War has already been referred to. Now those who were striving to raise interest in school education had to compete with a movement for political reform which took up much of the time and attention of the nation. Ever since the French Revolution there had been, in some political circles, a wariness about educating the poorer classes and so enabling them to become more articulate in voicing their demands. Even greater, however, was the fear of extending the franchise to people who might be wholly uneducated. This made more attractive the arguments of those who were in favor of a more comprehensive system of national education, particularly in England. It was, however, the Scottish Burgh Reform Act of 1833 which had the greatest impact on the Kirk and its work. Up until this time in many places the Burgh Council and the Kirk Session had been closely allied. Burgh schools, though provided by the burgh council, were often examined jointly with the presbytery. With the passing of the Burgh Reform Act councils now became more representative comprising a broad range of the middle class, including dissenters and radicals critical of the Church and less willing to work with it. There was a growing body of Protestant seceders who, uncomfortable with the system of patronage, were agitating for an end to all connection between church and state. Encouraged by the extension of the franchise the Edinburgh Voluntary Church Association had been set up early in 1833 to this end. The influence of the voluntaries, with their abhorrence of anything government supported, dissuaded some church members from supporting the work of a committee whose objective was to establish a church-controlled national system of school education. If, to the above concerns, were to be added other ongoing issues such as Poor Law Reform and Catholic Emancipation, both of which took up much of the time and energy of politicians and churchmen during these years, it can be seen that the Church's Education Committee was seeking support at a time of political and religious ferment when there was much to compete for the interest and backing of Church members and of the population at large.

IDENTIFYING FUTURE STRATEGIES

Within five years of the establishment of the first school the Education Committee had reached what was to be the optimum affordable number of schools for this decade. The early hope that within a short space of time over a hundred schools would be planted proved to be over ambitious. By 1830 eighty-six schools had been established. This was as many as the Church could safely provide for and the committee decided that the time had come to consolidate what had been achieved and that no more new schools could be considered in the meantime. This proved to be a realistic appraisal of the situation since, in spite of the apparent success of the new schools and the increase in numbers of pupils of all ages attending (from five to forty years of age), funding for the committee's work now tended to decrease rather than grow. An early sign of the committee's financial difficulties was its decision to turn down applications for schools even when these were accompanied by liberal offers of accommodation from the heritors. Income derived from congregational sources fluctuated from year to year and made budgeting difficult and the work of the committee would need to have been curtailed much sooner had it depended on these parish collections alone. As it was, year by year donations from benevolent societies and from individuals accounted for more than two-thirds of the committee's income. These and the interest from a Capital Fund of £5,000 set up from a private bequest helped to keep the committee afloat for a time but it was insufficient to provide for any extension of the work. The demand for additional schools continued to exceed what the committee could afford. In 1832 the committee had to appeal to parishes to help to clear the £500 deficit. It had been hoped that the Church's scheme for schooling in the Highlands would continue to be strenuously supported by the heritors, the clergy and the whole community of Scotland. Obviously such support had not been forthcoming. By 1834 with an estimated 80,000 people in the Highlands and Islands still unable to read and, according to its own calculations, almost 384 schools still required, the size of the problem seemed to have defeated the committee's most conscientious efforts. When it came to priorities ministers and congregations opted for the work of Church Extension. In 1834 parishes contributed £1,177 to the Education Committee's work while in 1835 £15,167 was gathered for the expansion of church accommodation.

In spite of the apparent lack of support from the parishes, the Education Committee continued to think creatively about the broader aspects and needs of school education. By 1834 it had identified two areas of development which it believed, could profitably be pursued namely government funding and teacher training. It was clear that the Assembly's contribution of eighty-six schools had only touched the surface of Scotland's problem. The Education Committee estimated that it required approximately £8,600 for the 384 schools still needed in the Highlands and Islands alone and not counting the schools desperately needed in the Central Belt. Facing what was more or less a moratorium on its own schools' programme, the committee turned its attention to another possible source of funding.

As we have seen in order to alleviate the want of churches in the Highlands, the Government had given a grant of £50,000 to build and endow forty-three new churches, aptly called "Parliamentary Churches"[18] and in May 1833 the General Assembly passed an Act providing these churches with *quoad sacra* parishes, that is, territorial districts over which the new churches would have spiritual jurisdiction. Recognizing that further expansion of schooling in Scotland under the supervision of the Church might be achieved through establishing schools in these newly created parishes, the Assembly of 1833 came up with the idea that the Church might apply to the Government for funding for that purpose. Noting that there were already indications that the Government was now prepared to allocate funding for the extension of education throughout the United Kingdom, the Church decided to petition the House of Commons for aid.[19] In making this application the committee was aware that in England to receive a grant towards the expense of maintaining a school, it was required that one half of the cost had to be defrayed by public subscription. Were this to apply in the Highlands, the public in Scotland would need to contribute upwards of £4,000.

All this time the Education Committee was all too aware of the plight of schooling in the Lowlands of Scotland. In the densely inhabited districts which should have been able to provide enough pupils to make them viable, the people were generally too poor to afford fees. In some instances the schools only opened in the winter because during the summer the teachers had to look around for more profitable work. In 1832 the committee outlined its plan for adopting such schools and appointing teachers who would be better paid and better qualified. The Assembly gave the committee authority to take the necessary steps to proceed with this plan but it was to be another five years before funds would be available for its implementation.

Early on the committee had recognized that the matter of teacher training would have to be taken seriously. In 1826 the committee had

18. The scheme was carried out between 1823 and 1830. Only thirty-two new churches and manses were built. They were designed by the Scottish architect and engineer Thomas Telford.

19. In 1833 Parliament voted £20,000 for the provision of schools in England and in 1834 set aside £10,000 for education in Scotland.

agreed that Assembly school teachers should be conversant with the best modern methods and so should spend time attending the Sessional school in Edinburgh. The Edinburgh Sessional School had first opened its doors in 1813 in Leith Wynd. It had started in 1812 as a Sabbath school established to take riotous and unruly youths off the Edinburgh streets and had subsequently been taken over as a day school by the kirk sessions in Edinburgh. In 1813 the management of the school was taken over by John Wood, an Episcopalian lawyer and Sheriff of Peebles, who had first taken an interest in the education of unemployed weavers. Woods was a born teacher and organizer and by 1824 the school had expanded and moved to Market Street where between 500 and 600 children were taught using the Madras monitorial system. Woods had established a widely admired curriculum and pedagogy and it was here that, by 1826, the Church had been sending its teachers for training. Nor was such training confined to new teachers, the committee expected teachers who were already in posts to accept in-service training during school holidays or at harvest time, presumably when many children would be working in the fields rather than attending school. From this time on the Church affirmed its faith in what it described as the "art of teaching" and in the need for "model" schools where teachers could receive practical training. It recommended schools in Arran and Tobermory in addition to the one in Edinburgh as model schools which teachers could attend for this purpose. It was also decided to set aside a school in Lerwick and establish it as a model school for Shetland where up until then school education had been more or less left to untrained boys and fishermen. In this way the Church pioneered teacher training and attempted to raise the standard of school education by equipping teachers both academically and practically for their profession. This was the beginning of an undertaking for which the Church would take responsibility up until the beginning of the twentieth century.

A DECISIVE YEAR

In many respects 1834 proved to be a watershed for the work of the Education Committee. It had reached a point where it could not proceed with new schools without further financial support and had been given the Assembly's backing to approach the Government for funding. As has been shown, its financial crisis was not helped by those who stepped up the campaign to increase church accommodation. In May 1834 under the leadership of Thomas Chalmers, the Church inaugurated a period of church-building activity with special collections and contributions being made by congregations all over the country. In the first year of the its existence Chalmers' committee raised £65,000, more than ten times what the Education Committee had raised in its first year. It was very apparent that church accommodation had a greater popular appeal than setting up schools. This disparity did not escape the notice of several presbyteries and a number formed themselves into associations to raise money for the work of the Church at home and abroad. Annual parish collections were pooled and the total was then divided up among the various schemes of the Church. The Presbytery of Edinburgh had been operating such a system since 1828. In the meantime the Education Committee had continued faithfully to keep the cause of school education before the nation and the *Scottish Guardian* newspaper was one of the first outside agencies to lend its support. In 1834 it helped to promote the founding of the Glasgow Educational Society (or Association) which advocated government funding for the extension of the parish school system under the control and supervision of the Established Church.[20] It was a report on the proceedings of a meeting of this Association at which George Lewis spoke on the "Extension of the Parochial Schools of Scotland," which formed the basis of his subsequent pamphlet, *Scotland a Half-Educated Nation*. Almost simultaneously J. C. Colquhoun, President of the Association, presented a Bill in Parliament to extend the provision for parish education in Scotland. In his speech to Parliament in 1834 Colquhoun argued that any government funding contributed towards Scottish education could be used to increase the salaries of schoolmasters rather than, as in England, applying the money to the erection of schools and schoolhouses. The General Assembly, he maintained, would have no trouble obtaining from heritors money for buildings if provision could be made for the masters. Colquhoun's Bill was thrown out mainly because the sum he had asked for (some £60,000) was considered excessive. If the amount he had proposed was necessary for education in Scotland, how much more, argued his fellow MPs, would be needed for England?

As the tenth anniversary of its formation approached the Education Committee could look back with pride on what it had achieved in promoting school education. It had courageously tackled the problem of

20. See Appendix 2.2.

education in remote areas and in Gaelic speaking communities. It had promoted the superintendence of schools by presbyteries and its convener and secretary had begun personally visiting schools, thus setting a precedent for school inspections. It had gained the respect and co-operation of heritors although this almost feudal dependence on the heritors may actually have acted as a disincentive to support from the Church at large. Still much remained to be done. Few of the poorly paid crofters and fishermen living in the scattered hamlets of the Highlands and Islands could afford the fees for good teachers or the cost of schoolbooks. Some, it was said, were willing to sell their best clothes to educate their children. Indeed, so anxious were the people for schooling that, according to Baird, it was not uncommon for a boy to be sent by the joint subscription of the poor inhabitants of the hamlets of a glen, to be boarded and educated at a distance, and for this boy on his return to become the schoolmaster of his neighborhood. In 1833 it estimated that out of a total population in the Highlands and Islands of over 500,000 the number still not able to read was about 83,000 (over 28,000 of those being between six and twenty years of age) and that to ensure that the population in that part of Scotland could read in either Gaelic or English, there would need to be 384 additional schools. It was calculated that even offering a salary as low as £20 per annum, the committee would require £7,680 for salaries and a further £1,000 for other necessary expenditure. It was evident that the Church was never going to be able to complete this task on its own and that any further expansion of the committee's work would be very limited without substantial financial help from outside. Moreover it had to act soon if it was going to preserve and extend its control of a national system of school education. The opposition of an increasing number of schools set up by dissenters and Catholics outside the oversight of the Established Church was a factor which the Kirk could no longer afford to ignore. It was time to appeal to the government.

Appendix 2.1

THOMAS CHALMERS (1780–1847) WAS the first Moderator of the Free Church of Scotland which was formed at the Disruption in 1843. In 1819 he became minister of the church and parish of St John in Glasgow. Initially he set up two schools with four teachers attended by seven hundred children. Between forty and fifty local Sabbath schools were opened, where more than a thousand children were taught the elements of secular and religious education. David Stow (1793–1864) was involved in Sunday School teaching which convinced him of the importance of effective training for teachers at all levels. In 1827 Stow set up his first school in Glasgow. In 1836 he established a school for teacher training. Following the Disruption of 1843, a legal ruling of 1845 held that the school was part of the Church of Scotland. Stow and most of his colleagues who were adherents of the Free Church of Scotland were compelled to resign from what had become state-funded teaching posts. Stow established a new college in Glasgow as the Free Church Normal Seminary.

Appendix 2.2

PRINCIPLES AND RULES OBSERVED BY THE COMMITTEE IN THE ESTABLISHING OF SCHOOLS

I. That no School shall be established in any parish which has not already a Parochial School regularly endowed and supported agreeably to Act of Parliament.

II. That no School shall he fixed at a station so near the Parochial School as to enterfere [sic] with the usual attendance, or to injure the interests of its master.

III. For every stationary or permanent school, a suitable, well aired and lighted school-room, with the requisite forms and tables, and a dwelling house of not less than two rooms for the teacher, together with a kailyard, and a croft of land sufficient for the maintenance of a cow, both summer and winter; and also the necessary fuel, or a proper compensation in lieu of these latter accommodations—must be provided by the proprietors or inhabitants of the district.

IV. That Schools shall be permanently stationed at such places as can furnish regularly a sufficient and steady number of Scholars, and that there shall be alternating or itinerating Schools in those districts which do not furnish so many Scholars as seem necessary to justify the cost of a permanent establishment, and in which, it would be less easy to obtain a grant of the accommodations.

HEADS OF REGULATIONS TO BE FOLLOWED BY TEACHERS IN CONDUCTING THEIR SCHOOLS

I. The teacher shall uniformly open and close his school with prayer every day.

II. He shall call over a roll of his scholars every day; mark those who are absent, that he may take the best means of ascertaining the cause of their having been absent, and keep an accurate record of such absences, that he may be able to report distinctly and correctly to the Committee, from time to time, as to the degree of attendance given by each of his scholars.

III. He shall teach the school—hours every day, during summer, and—during winter, except on Saturday, when he shall not be requested to teach above hours.

IV. He shall be entitled to demand fees from the scholars, in all cases in which the Minister and Kirk-session do not certify that they are unable to pay them; but these fees shall in no case exceed the average of those that are paid at the parish school.

V. He shall not be at liberty to introduce any book into his school, except such as have been previously approved of, and authorized by the Committee.

VI. He shall cause the younger scholars to learn the Mother's Catechism, together with a verse of a Psalm, Paraphrase, or passage of Scripture, as soon as they are able to read these; and, as they advance, the Shorter Catechism with proofs, every day; which exercise they shall repeat on Saturday.

VII. He shall prescribe portions of the Psalms and Paraphrases, or passages of Scripture, every Saturday to the scholars, according to the progress they have made, which they shall be required to commit to memory, and to repeat on Monday.

VIII. When the Scriptures, or portions of them, are read or repeated, he shall be most careful that the scholars do so reverently; and he shall not allow them to trap one another, or lose and gain places, when they are employed in these solemn exercises.

IX. He shall anxiously endeavour to explain to his scholars what they read or repeat, by putting suitable questions to them, as to the meaning of the words and sentiments expressed in it; and shall make it his special study to do so, particularly in regard to religion and moral duties.

X. He shall, every half year, report to the Committee the state of his school, viz. the names and number of scholars that have entered and been in attendance—their age—the specific number of days they have been present or absent—the progress they had made before entering, and the progress they have made in their respective classes, during the half year—the individuals who have particularly distinguished themselves in the different branches of education, and by their general good conduct, &c. With this view he shall be furnished by the Committee with printed forms, or tables, which he shall carefully fill up, and transmit to the Committee, on the 1st days of April and October.

XI. The vacation shall not exceed six weeks in any one year.

Appendix 2.3

A T A MEETING OF the Glasgow Educational Society held in Glasgow, 24th February, 1834, Henry Dunlop, Esq. of Craigton in the Chair, it was unanimously resolved:

1. That our freedom, our loyalty, our peace and plenty, our social comfort, and our national renown, arise from the intellectual, the moral, and above all, from the religious character, of our countrymen; and that a system of national education, on Scriptural principles, in connexion with the religious institutions of Scotland, and commensurate with the wants of the population, is essential to the perpetuity of our national prosperity.

2. That whilst Scotland, since the Union, has increased above twofold in population, and a hundredfold in wealth, no adequate provision has been made, out of her increasing wealth, for the education of her increasing population. The number of Parochial Schools remains nearly the same as at the period of the Union; and including schools of all sorts, national, charity, and private, there is good reason apprehend, that both the city and rural population of Scotland, but especially the former, are lamentably destitute of the means of efficient education, and that Scotland both in the quantity and quality of her educational institutions, is falling behind other European nations.

3. That this Meeting, calling to mind the unwearied efforts of the Church and nation of Scotland, in an early and barbarous age, and the precedence which this country long enjoyed, as an educated nation, desire to respond to the call of the present Lord Chancellor of England, who at the recent Wilberforce meeting at York, is reported to have said, ". . . that the efforts of the people were still wanting to promote education and that Parliament would do nothing until they themselves took the matter in hand with energy and spirit, and with the determination to do something," in obedience to this call, as well as to a higher sense of duty in this important mat-

ter, this Meeting resolve itself into an Association for the extension and improvement of the means of sound and efficient popular instruction.

4. That the objects of the Association shall be to obtain and diffuse information regarding the popular schools of our own and other countries—their excellencies and defects—to awaken their countrymen to the wants of Scotland in particular—to procure petitions to the legislature soliciting parliamentary inquiry, and parliamentary aid, in behalf of the extension of the Parochial Schools, with such additional institutions and improvements as the present state of society in our cities, and recent advances in the art of instruction, may suggest or require.

The Church of Scotland Magazine No. II, vol. I, April 1834, 50.

3

The Cost of Progress

THE FIRST PARLIAMENTARY GRANTS

BY 1834 IT HAD become clear that the eighty-six schools which the Assembly's committee had been responsible for setting up had made little impact on the needs of the Highlands and had been of very little benefit to the rest of the country. Many localities still lacked any kind of educational provision. In addition the salaries and conditions of schoolmasters did nothing to make the teaching profession more attractive. The passing of the Chapels Act in 1834 and the national church extension campaign had created new quoad sacra parishes in the Lowlands and "government church" parishes in the Highlands. These only served to emphasize the gaps in the parish educational provision. Funding had to be found for schools in these new parishes since the statutory legislation regarding the obligations of heritors did not apply. It was evident that in the Scotland of the nineteenth century the old feudal-like system which depended on heritors providing for parish schools and schoolmasters was no longer appropriate or adequate. The pressing need for more schools was highlighted by the irregularity of pupils' attendance often due to the distances that had to be traveled. To try and overcome this evening classes were opened for children working in factories or in the fields, but pupils were often so tired that they were unable to learn very much. It appeared that the only answer would have been an act enforcing at least part-time compulsory attendance. Books and equipment were a costly but necessary provision. In many cases parents either refused to pay for these or could not afford to buy them. In 1835 the *Scotsman* newspaper quoted David Welsh, professor of Ecclesiastical

History at Edinburgh, as remarking in an Assembly debate that he had been in schools where, "there was only one book in the whole school; and he knew one where there were only two books, namely, the Proverbs of Solomon, and a tract on the Corn Laws." Circulating libraries had to be restocked. Sometimes the schoolmaster was given authority to sell school books to pupils at reduced prices but normally text books were shared by children from poorer backgrounds. As a result there were greater demands on congregations and on other independent providers. In the towns and cities church members contributed to various private endeavors and local churches attempted to help in different ways. In the city of Glasgow Sessional schools under the control of the kirk sessions were largely supported from congregational givings and served as parish schools. School buildings and the housing for schoolmasters were paid for out of session funds. In Edinburgh the Governors of George Heriot's Hospital regularly set aside considerable portions of its revenues for the elementary education of the poor. In 1837 the School Accommodation Society of Greenock was set up to meet the educational needs of the considerable population of poor Highlanders living there, and on the Moray Firth the Society of the Respectable Inhabitants of Nairn helped with the education of the fishing population of that town. In Glasgow a number of schools were supported by commercial businesses. Messrs. Denniston, Buchanan and Company, for example, provided a school and a school house and a salary of £20 for a teacher and James Finlay and Company paid a teacher £20 to provide two hours of education during the day and £50 to run an evening school for young adults who were employed in the cotton mills. Presbyterial Associations worked hard to raise money for all four of the great schemes of the Church. Individual church members were encouraged to join penny-a-week subscription schemes similar to those introduced by the Church Extension Committee. Landowners formed County Associations to provide voluntary contributions for schools in their own districts. By this time presbyteries were much more attentive in their supervision of schools to the extent that it could be claimed that a statutory form of national inspection of schools was in force long before the appointment of Government inspectors but given the limited powers and resources of presbyteries to make any real changes, it is debatable how effective such inspections really were.

Despite continuous appeals and inducements (in 1837 the committee actually promised any contributor donating £500 or £600 the privilege of deciding where a school should be located) a note of despair was often heard in the committee's reports to the General Assembly. Unable to provide sufficient funding from church contributions for all it would like to have undertaken, the committee decided to follow up the two objectives which it had previously identified, both of which meant obtaining Government finance. One was to persuade the Government to grant assistance for schools in the densely populated towns and cities in the Lowlands and in the quoad sacra parishes of the Parliamentary Churches in the Highlands. The other was to put teacher training on a firmer basis by establishing Normal schools.[1] At its meeting in May 1835 the General Assembly gave its full support to the committee's proposals and agreed to petition the House of Commons for aid. It was the committee's hope that while it could not afford to set up new schools in the new industrial townships, it could try to raise the standard of the existing schooling by improving the qualifications of schoolmasters and supplementing their salaries. It believed that this would encourage teachers to stay longer in the one school rather than look for better prospects elsewhere and that continuity and better teaching would make schooling more attractive and effective. Professor David Welsh, in supporting the committee, entertained the Assembly with his descriptions of some schools he had known where children were taught by disbanded soldiers, disabled sailors, by shepherds, and by ploughmen and he had known some instances of persons being appointed to teach in a school on the strength of certificates from their former employers, "given, not because their former employers were satisfied of their excellence, but because they wished to get rid of them as nuisances."[2]

In anticipation of receiving Government grants for extending school education in terms of their proposals, the committee drafted a new set of Rules and Regulations. These outlined their plans for augmenting the salaries of teachers and stipulated that preference would be given to districts where the people were poorest both in the Highlands and Islands and

---

1. The name was derived from the French "école normalle." It was a school which would establish standards for the teaching profession. Later these would be known as teacher training colleges.

2. Welsh was one of the founders of the Glasgow Infant School Society. In this capacity he is likely to have had an intimate knowledge of elementary schools. Given his involvement with the Society's model school in Glasgow, he would have a special interest in a model School in Edinburgh. *Scotsman*, 26 May, 1835.

in the large towns, on the condition that any parish where an Assembly school was established would be required to transmit annually a collection to the general fund of the committee. With regard to the new schoolmasters and teachers who might be recruited nothing was said about church membership. The only requirements were that they should have a competent knowledge Christianity and continue the traditional practice of opening and closing the school with prayer, teaching the Catechism, and reading and explaining a portion of the Scriptures daily. The appointment and dismissal of all teachers employed under this scheme would belong exclusively to the committee.

For the government the question of subsidizing education was not clear cut. It was now confronted almost contemporaneously with the needs of the three countries, Scotland, England and Ireland, and here the involvement of religious interests complicated the situation. It was not just a matter of finding and allocating funding, nor was it just a case of identifying the most deserving, it was a question of how appropriate it was to use taxpayers' money to support church bodies who were responsible for schools and who had a particular interest in religious instruction, and which of these bodies to support. The main division of opinion was not between religious education and secular education, but between two different notions of religious education. One opinion favored a general and simple education in religion without any instruction characteristic of a particular church's creed or liturgy. The other opinion held that religious instruction was useless unless it included training in the beliefs and doctrines of the denomination which had sponsored the school. When it came to the Church of Scotland's application for grants this matter of religious instruction was less of an issue. The Church had always been proud of the fact that pupils of all denominations were treated equally and were welcome in all schools under its supervision including the parish schools. Teachers were directed not to press on Catholic children any instruction to which their parents or their priest might object and allowances were made for Catholic parents to withdraw their children from religious instruction if they so wished. Moreover the committee were always anxious to point out that the education delivered in the Assembly schools was comprehensive and secular enough to allow many of the scholars to leave their traditional family occupations and set out on new careers. In its reports the committee carefully balanced the moral benefits with the educational benefits of its schools. The committee could point to various careers taken up by former pupils—manufacturing businesses in the large towns, masters of sailing ships, adventure teachers—but was circumspect enough to add, "religion, it must be remembered, is a principal and over-ruling element in the plainest education given at the assembly schools." As if to underline its point in 1836 the Education Committee seems to have changed its official designation without ever reporting that it had done so. Whereas up until then it had been called the "Committee of the General Assembly for increasing the *means of Education and Religious Instruction* [my italics] in Scotland particularly in the Highlands and Islands," from 1836 it was called the "Committee of the General Assembly for increasing *the means of Education* in Scotland particularly in the Highlands and Islands"—the phrase "and Religious Instruction" having been dropped from the title. However in its appeal to the church-going public at large the committee made sure that it retained its emphasis on the need for religious and moral education in all schools throughout Scotland.

Negotiations with the government finally produced results and in 1834 Scotland received £10,000 as its share of a Parliamentary grant to national education. In 1836 and again in 1837 further Government grants of £10,000 were made for the erection of school-houses and for the edu-cation of the children from the poorer classes in the densely populated Scottish towns. A substantial proportion of these grants went towards the upkeep of sessional schools. Of the £10,000 granted by Parliament in 1837, £6,000 was to be used to set up endowments for schoolmasters in each of the Parliamentary Church parishes in the Highlands. This was the first time grants had been made towards schoolmasters' salaries. This allocation, however, was hardly generous. It was calculated that invested at 3½ percent, £6,000 would only provide nine or ten salaries, still leaving another thirty-one to be provided for.

By this time the presbyteries throughout the land were beginning to wake up to the way things were going and there were growing fears that it was only a matter of time before the Government would lay down condi-tions which would accompany any further grant and which would threaten the Church's control of schools. Behind this anxiety was a dispute which had nothing to do with school education. With the growing strength of the evangelical wing of the Church had come increasing opposition to the power of the heritors as patrons presenting ministers to parishes and the belief that congregations should have a greater say in the appointment of ministers. In 1834 the General Assembly had passed the Veto Act which had restricted the operation of patronage and given a greater voice to congregations in the selection of ministers. In some cases, however, the wishes of the people had been overruled by the Court of Session and the Veto Act set aside. The House of Lords as the supreme court in the land had ruled in favor of the patron and against the decisions of the General Assembly. This was in essence the dispute which would grow and erupt in 1843 and result in the Disruption. When it came to education some in the Church believed that if the state could intervene in these appointments how far might it, as paymaster, seek to dictate policy and appointments in schools. There was a flurry of petitions and overtures from presbyteries calling on the General Assembly to secure the Church's traditional rights over the control of schooling in Scotland but it was now too late to turn the clock back. In May 1838 following yet another Parliamentary inquiry into the state of education in Scotland, the Highland Schools Act (An Act to facilitate the Foundation and Endowment of Additional Schools in Scotland) was passed with the government laying down the salary scales for teachers in schools in the newly erected government parishes in the Highlands. The passing of this Act coincided more or less with the set- ting up of a new Privy Council committee in April 1839, the Committee of Council on Education, "to superintend the application of any sums voted by Parliament for the purpose of promoting Public Education." From now on this committee would be responsible for the allocation of grants for school education in Scotland and England and for determining the conditions on which these grants would be made. Soon after it was constituted the Committee of Council made it known that the right of in- spection would be one of the conditions accompanying any future grants. It also had to be satisfied that no other funds were available and that a school-house had been obtained. At the same time the new Council tried to anticipate any opposition by making it clear that inspectors would have no powers to interfere with religious instruction or the management and discipline of schools or to suggest changes which the managers of schools would be disinclined to make. It was to be the chief role and object of the inspectors to collect facts and information. These latter reassurances were not heard in Scotland. Almost immediately synods and presbyteries in Scotland began to voice their objections and express their fears for the future of religious education which for them meant instruction in the Bible and in the doctrines of the Westminster Confession of Faith. There was also concern that any government inspection of schools would clash with the authority of presbyterial superintendence and inspections. In answering a letter from the Education Committee requesting clarification of the new regulations and in particular how the Privy Council intended to cooperate with the Church of Scotland, the secretary James Phillips Kay (who later preferred to be known as James Kay-Shuttleworth) sought to reassure the Church that the Committee of Council would at all times cooperate with the Assembly's Committee and would consult it with regard to the selection of inspectors. With regard to its policy of appointing inspectors to Scottish schools, the Committee of Council assured the Church that it would select "gentlemen who possess the confidence of the Church of Scotland" and who would appreciate the church's aims in providing elementary education for those in the poorer class. These reassurances seem to have satisfied the committee and after a heated discussion the General Assembly agreed by 157 votes to 105 to accept the Council's conditions. This was a major concession on the part of the Church and an acknowledgement that it could no longer afford to be independent. Yet in another sense it was an indication of the Church's confidence in its reputation and standing in this field and in the quality and importance of the Education Committee's work. The committee certainly believed that its policy and achievements made it a worthy partner of the Government and that, with the force of the ancient statutes behind it, it was in a strong enough position to hold its own in any disputes.

The Church had been promised that inspectors would only be interested in collecting facts and that they would not interfere with the running of the schools. This was an understatement to say the least. The so-called "collecting of facts" turned out to be very thorough and covered every aspect of school life. In a section of the Committee of Council minutes for 1840 headed "Instructions For The Inspection of Schools" it was laid down that inspectors were expected to report on the living conditions of schoolmasters, the books used, the layout of classrooms, the way the teaching was organized and the methods used, means of discipline and punishment, school attendance, and the targets and attainments of pupils in a wide range of subjects. Where schools were connected with the Church, inspectors were to explore how far the doctrines and principles of the Church were instilled into the minds of the children. Any application for a grant towards building a new school had to be accompanied by detailed plans of its dimensions and provision. An inspection of schools in the Presbyteries of Haddington and Dunbar carried out in

June 1841 by HM Inspector of Schools John Gibson gives us some insight into what a typical visit involved. The inspection lasted just over six weeks and included parish schools, burgh schools, endowed schools, adventure schools, and female schools, sixty-four schools in all. Gibson's report included details of the situation and size of school buildings, whether children were assembled and dismissed with prayer and the Bible read, the subjects taught and the books used for lessons. He remarked on the irregularity of attendance and suggested that proper registers should be kept. He noted that there was a need for good but inexpensive school-books and that generally speaking school accommodation was unsatisfactory. On the whole teachers in parish schools came out best while teachers in side schools and adventure schools were reported as being the most ineffective and least well qualified. Reflecting on the latter he commented, "The education of a great proportion of our population rests on a precarious, unsatisfactory, and infirm basis." In many respects this report was not significantly different from the kind of reports which had been regularly prepared by presbyteries for the Assembly's Education Committee. Apart from gleaning information about developments in different parts of the country and being able to offer advice and share ideas, it was not clear at this stage what the Committee of Council intended to do with the facts it was collecting or how far these would be used to influence its funding decisions.

While it was true that from now on schools in Scotland receiving Exchequer grants would be open to HM Inspectors in addition to Presbytery examination, as yet this posed no real threat to the Church's authority. Any fears regarding the removal of religious instruction in schools proved groundless. Indeed, the fact that this was one of the subjects to be inspected, confirmed its place in the school curriculum. This did not seem to satisfy everyone in the Kirk. Expressions of concern continued not for school education in general, but rather for the future of religious instruction, especially instruction in the Protestant faith and about the Church of Scotland. It did not seem to be important to these protesters that government grants and inspection might benefit Scottish education as a whole.

On 14 January 1840, Principal Baird, the first convener of the Education Committee, died at the age of seventy-eight. Baird was the person who initially had drawn the Church's attention to the serious state of education in the Highlands and Islands and had been the driving force behind the committee since its inception in 1825. In assessing the needs of the country he had not been content to draw conclusions only on the basis of submitted reports, but at great personal inconvenience and in a time of poor health, he had, on at least two occasions, toured the Highlands from Argyll and Kintyre to Lewis and Orkney and Shetland, surveying the situation for himself. In doing this he had set an example to future HMI John Gordon, the committee secretary, and other committee members, demonstrating how useful such an independent inspection of schools could be. Baird's death coincided with the end of one era and the beginning of another in the Established Church's relationship with school education in Scotland.

THE EXTENSION OF TEACHER TRAINING

The Church's First Normal School

The success of Mr. Wood's Sessional School in Edinburgh had persuaded the Education Committee to insist that before taking up their posts all teachers should spend time there and familiarize themselves with up-to-date teaching methods. By this time the Church was beginning to take seriously the need for the professional training of schoolmasters. There was concern that there was no required course of study and no standard qualifications for teachers as there were for other professions. The original intention of Wood's school had been to improve the standard of teaching in the subjects commonly taught in elementary schools. The committee now were of the opinion that the church should have its own Model School to cope with increasing numbers of teachers and to offer more advanced training. In 1835 the Education Committee proposed that initially training would be of two standards. Those being trained in subjects taught at "the higher class of schools" (parish schools, burgh schools, and privately endowed schools) would attend for two years, while those expecting to take up posts where only the three Rs were taught, would only be required to attend for eighteen months. Existing teachers who wished to take advantage of this training were to be admitted at any age and all those who completed their course would receive a diploma certifying their qualifications. At first teachers were slow to take advantage of the training available, but gradually the numbers increased. Even short periods of training were seen to be beneficial. In 1836 the Assembly learned that Wood's Sessional School would now be known as the General Assembly's

Normal Seminary in Edinburgh. In the following year negotiations were completed for the hand-over of the property and the superintendence of the school to the Assembly's committee on the understanding that each of the Edinburgh Kirk Sessions would have the privilege of sending twelve children for education in the school gratis, or at such rates as the respective sessions thought appropriate and that it would continue as a school for the education of poor children.

With the increasing emphasis on teacher training the duration and content of the prescribed courses had to be brought up-to-date. To enter a Normal school candidates who intended to teach in Assembly schools had to sit an entrance examination and were expected to display an aptitude for teaching. Those who could not afford the entrance fee were exempt and the committee contributed towards their keep. They were expected to have a connection with the Church of Scotland, but those not seeking employment by the Church were not asked about their religious affiliation. The committee stated that the length of attendance was never prescribed and depended on the knowledge and skills acquired before starting the training course and the type of school students hoped to teach in. It varied from one to ten or twelve months but seldom was longer than six months. Those training for Church of Scotland schools had to stay on until the staff were satisfied with their performance. They then received a certificate of fitness. Others could leave when they wished, usually without a certificate showing their qualifications. It would appear that the actual period of attendance varied considerably. HMI Gibson on his visit to the Presbytery of Tain noted that five out of the seven Assembly teachers had been trained in the Edinburgh Normal School. One had attended for more than two years, another for eighteen months, and another for only four months, while of the others some had received only two months training.

The duration of courses would soon become a matter of dispute with the Committee of Council, the Church believing that the training of its teachers had to be tailored to suit the kind of posts they would be taking up in rural and urban situations. The standard curriculum covered the three *R*s as well as the elements of science, English composition, geography and religious instruction. (Subsequently, in 1843, the Assembly would instruct the committee to include instruction in reading music for the promotion of psalmody in schools.) Evidently, although Latin and Greek were taught in a number of schools, they were not seen as particularly useful subjects as far as future employment was concerned. Students at Glasgow and Edinburgh continued to receive their practical training in the Model Schools which were run in conjunction with the Normal schools at both locations and which were attended by some five to six hundred children from the poorer classes in those cities. In the years 1835–1836 there were only twenty-seven teachers in training at Edinburgh and of these fifteen had been placed by the committee. By 1839 the number had risen to 122 and soon the demand for trained teachers outstripped supply.

Further Developments

There was now a good case for extending this provision and in the summer of 1840 the Education Committee wrote to the Committee of Council exploring the possibility of funding for the erection of a new Normal school building in Edinburgh and for a grant to cover its maintenance. In considering this request the Committee of Council had to take into account discussions it had been having with the Glasgow Educational Society. This society had been set up to manage the Model Schools which David Stow had pioneered in Glasgow. By 1839 the Society was heavily in debt, mainly as a result of undertaking the erection of its new Normal school at Dundas Vale which had been opened in 1837 but was not yet completed. In spite of substantial Treasury grants, by 1841 the debt stood at £11,000 and there seemed little hope of the society ever clearing this.

Before investing further Government money in a scheme which, although offering valuable training for future teachers, appeared to be a financial disaster, the Committee of Council decided to send HMI John Gibson to Glasgow to inspect the school. In his report back to the Council Gibson expressed concern at the standard of students being accepted for training. He claimed that almost any boy or girl of thirteen or fourteen years of age could meet the entrance requirements. Those enrolled the previous year had been a motley collection. One had been a Church of Scotland minister, one had been a carpenter, one a dancing teacher, one a portrait painter, one a baker, three had been shopkeepers, and twenty-one had been teachers from small adventure schools. Gibson concluded that the training received at the Glasgow Normal School was totally inadequate and contrasted unfavorably with that provided by the Assembly's Normal School in Edinburgh.

By the summer of 1841 therefore the Council had before it both an application for funding from the Church of Scotland and a further application from the struggling Glasgow Education Society. Not wishing to lose the benefits of the Glasgow Normal School, the Council sent Gibson back to Scotland later that year with the instruction that he was to confer with both the directors of the Society and representatives of the General Assembly's Education Committee. As a result a plan was drawn up whereby the Glasgow institution would be placed under the direct control of the Church's Education Committee in return for a grant which would go towards building and running a new Normal school in Edinburgh and also towards paying off the debt incurred by the Glasgow Educational Society. It was agreed that the Committee of Council would give £5,000 to be used to defray a portion of the debt incurred by the Glasgow Educational Society on condition that the Education Committee would be responsible for the remainder of the debt and that the Glasgow Educational Society would hand over the buildings at Dundas Vale to be maintained by the Church as an elementary school for the children of the poor in the city of Glasgow and as a Normal school for the instruction and training of schoolmasters. The Council also agreed to give the Church a further grant of £5,000 on the condition that the General Assembly raise another £5,000 and that the total (£10,000) be used to pay for schools for the children of the poor in Edinburgh and for a new Normal school building. In both Glasgow and Edinburgh the right of the Government to inspect all schools was secured. It was calculated that £1,000 (a £500 annual Government grant and a £500 subsidy from the Church) together with fees and subscriptions, would pay for the running of these establishments. One important stipulation made by the Council was that its £5,000 contribution for the Edinburgh building would not be paid until the building had actually been erected. There were a number of other conditions stated in the terms of acceptance which would later become matters of contention. The first was that if it seemed to the Committee of Council that the Normal schools were not being maintained and conducted satisfactorily by the Church, the annual payments of £500 would be stopped. Secondly, a rector was to be appointed in each establishment and the Committee of Council was to have a say in the appointments made and could at any time withdraw their approval of a rector or headmaster who then must resign. The Church's committee did not object to the Council having a say in the appointment of a rector but took exception to the latter part of the clause arguing that it involved an interference with, and control over, the management and discipline of the school. This was held by the Education Committee to contradict an existing agreement set down in a communication of July 1840 from the Committee of Council which stated that there would be no interference in the management or discipline of the schools. The Council agreed to withdraw this condition and in May 1842 the General Assembly accepted the Committee of Council's proposals and urged its Education Committee to set about raising its share of the costs without delay. In a letter sent in November 1842 to the committee, it was made clear that the Committee of Council regarded the building of the new school in Edinburgh and the take-over of the school in Glasgow as all part of the one plan and so any grant depended on the fulfilment of both parts of the agreement. The Church did not see it that way and the dispute over the terms of the original agreement rumbled on for years. In 1848 following an HMI report on Scotland's Normal schools the Committee of Council decided to withhold its annual grant of £500 to the Glasgow school. It maintained that the situation in Glasgow did not merit the grant as no rector had been appointed since 1845 when the committee had taken over the management of the school. The Committee of Council argued that without a rector the school at Glasgow could not be run properly and referred back to the original agreement which stated that where either of the schools was not managed to the Council's satisfaction the annual payments could be withheld. For its part the committee claimed that it had never understood that the financial arrangements for both schools were to be regarded as part of the one plan and that even without a rector, the school in Glasgow was well run and well taught.

The disputes and uncertainties before and after the Disruption meant that the years 1842–1844 were not the best of times to be trying to raise money from congregations. By April 1843 subscriptions towards the new Edinburgh school only amounted to £1,600 and a proportion of this was conditional on there being no secession. The committee was therefore far short of its target of £5,000. The Church's failure to raise its share of the £10,000 total had meant that the scheme to build the Edinburgh school was held up. This in turn meant that the Committee of Council refused to advance the Church any money since it regarded the two schemes (for Glasgow and Edinburgh) as part of the one plan. The Church protested vehemently but eventually had to climb down and assure the Council that the plans for both schools would proceed. In its correspondence the Council never mentioned the Disruption nor conceded that the turmoil congregations were going through might have been an explanation for the Church's financial shortfall.

By September 1843 partly as a result of losing the support of members who had joined the Free Church, the Education Committee was left with only £1,000 to put towards the cost of the new school in Edinburgh. Concluding that the necessary £5,000 was well beyond its reach, the committee went back to the Committee of Council with the suggestion that the projected cost of the new building should be reduced and that the committee and the Council should now each contribute £2,500. The Council agreed but stipulated that the new school must be adequate to meet their requirements which included accommodation for two hundred children in the Model School. The Education Committee accepted the Council's conditions and proceeded to commission the building of the new Edinburgh school at a cost of £8,000. The opening ceremony took place on 19 May 1845, with the building free of debt.[3]

During these negotiations and in the years following, the Education Committee seems to have gone on with its plans regardless of the great dispute which was splitting the Church. The atmosphere of bitterness and hostility meant that there was little concern that most of the staff of the Glasgow Normal School would secede to the Free Church and lose their jobs and that founding members such as David Stow and Professor David Welsh, both of whom had gone over to the Free Church, would be sacrificing a dream they had worked long and hard to realize. The committee believed rather naively that it would soon fill the posts vacated by those who joined the Free Church and that its schools would continue to operate very much as they had always done and would be acceptable to every denomination. In reality the effect of the Disruption on the Established Church's educational scheme was greater than it cared to admit. It lost the use of the schools and schoolmasters' houses which had been provided by heritors who seceded to the Free Church. Half of the teachers in Assembly schools left voluntarily or were dismissed when they went over to the Free Church, and the Church lost its right to examine more than three hundred others who were sympathetic to Free Church principles.[4] Perhaps

3. This building known as the Church of Scotland Normal and Sessional School was sited in Johnston Terrace.

4. The actual numbers of teachers who had to relinquish their posts in Assembly schools as a result of the Disruption is variously reported by the different churches and

most seriously of all the Disruption weakened the Kirk's claim to be the national Church with statutory oversight of parish schools. In spite of these difficulties in May 1845 the Normal School in Glasgow was opened under the management of the Established Church and the Church decided that no teacher would be appointed to an Assembly school who had not undergone a period of training at one or other of its Normal schools. In the face of competition from the Free Church, by 1849 the number of Assembly schools rose from 146 in 1843 before the Disruption to 208, 58 of these in Lowland parishes[5]

GOVERNMENT FUNDING 1845–49

Grants to Normal Schools

In February 1845 HMI John Gibson produced a highly critical report on the state of Scottish schools. It made reference to the fact that the Church of Scotland's aims for extending the provision of school education lay far beyond its means and there was still a dire shortage of parish schools especially in small and scattered rural communities. In particular Gibson's report highlighted the inadequate salaries being paid to teachers. He reckoned that a salary of £35 was not enough to attract a good teacher yet in almost two thousand parishes throughout the country it was less. In fact the average income for a schoolmaster was still only about £19. Around the same time similar reports were being submitted by inspectors in England. It was clear that Government intervention was called for on a national scale. Consequently just as the Established Church's Normal schools were beginning to pick up following the difficult years of the Disruption, they were faced with problems arising from the Committee of Council's decision to introduce a new scheme for funding parish schools and schoolmasters and Normal schools.

In June 1847 the committee was informed that instead of annual grants to Normal schools, it would receive an allowance for each student enrolled and that the amount would vary depending on how long the

equally variously interpreted by historians. The accuracy of the count is not helped by the fact that some chose to count parish and Church of Scotland Assembly teachers as Church of Scotland teachers while others count them separately.

5. By 1849 the Free Church had 428 schools fully supported by church funds, and two Normal schools, one in Glasgow and one in Edinburgh.

student attended the school. In addition there would now be a category of students called Queen's Scholars, being those who had first of all successfully passed through an apprenticeship in parish and subscription schools. The cost of training these was to be shared by the Government and spread over three years. The Kirk's Education Committee protested that this new scheme would be unworkable since often a student's course had to be terminated to allow him to take up a teaching post which had to be filled. Vacancies could occur at any time and the committee was obliged to fill them with teachers who might have attended a Normal school for only a few months, but were otherwise academically qualified. For the committee to depart from this practice and enforce periods of attendance from one to three years would seriously harm elementary education in Scotland. Where students stayed for only a year or less the committee would lose whatever remuneration would have been paid to them in their second and third years. There was no alternative but to reject the Privy Council's proposals. This led to yet another head-on clash with the Council and the start of an acrimonious correspondence of charge and counter-charge which lasted over a number of months. The Council complained that it was spending more money in Scotland than in England but the Church countered this by claiming that there were statistics to show that the Scottish system of training teachers was much superior. The Committee of Council accused the Education Committee of failing to ensure that its Normal schools fulfilled the objects for which they had been set up and for which they had been financially supported by the Government, and in reply the committee protested that the London-based Council did not understand that its schools were specifically designed to meet the particular needs of school education in Scotland. The committee argued that if teachers were too well trained they were likely to be less willing to take up posts in the remote rural areas where all that was required was to offer a basic education which would at least enable people to count and to read the Bible. The Committee of Council's response was that in proposing the new financial arrangements it was only trying to increase the income of the Normal schools. At present it gave £500 per annum to the Edinburgh school. By subsidizing the students individually, including the Queen's scholars, the grant could come to between £1,200 and £1,500. It also pointed out that some thirteen years previously, in 1835, the Education Committee had itself stated its intention that training would be offered for two distinct classes of teachers—one for the elementary schools, the other for those who might teach at a more advanced level. In reply the Education Committee claimed that the Privy Council had no power to dictate to the Church what curriculum it should follow or to prescribe a minimum period of attendance. Courses had to be tailored to suit the kinds of situations teachers would be facing in town and country. It argued that to insist on teachers undertaking courses lasting up to three years would change the whole nature of Normal schools and turn them into colleges of education. Education in its broader, more formal sense was the task of universities, which in Scotland were open to all, whereas the main function of the Church's Normal schools was training in teaching skills. There was also the fear that, under the Committee of Council's new scheme for the introduction of monitors or apprentice teachers in parish schools, Normal schools would be put out of business. As a result of pressure from the Church the Council eventually dropped its proposals and agreed to fund Normal schools according to the existing arrangements.

Undoubtedly the Government recognized the value of the pioneering work which the Church had done and was willing to encourage and subsidize its growth. Unfortunately the more ambitious the committee was to extend its provision, the more it became financially dependent on the Government, which in turn was in a stronger position to dictate conditions and policy. The problem was that the Government was dealing with issues at a United Kingdom level and the Church objected to measures which seemed inappropriate to the Scottish situation.

Concern for Schoolmasters

The same accusation was leveled at the Government when it came to dealing with the conditions and salaries of schoolmasters. With its involvement in planting schools and in teacher training it was natural that the Church should maintain an interest in their payment. In 1834 it had supported the Scottish schoolmasters' petition which asked the Government to raise salaries by the value of one chalder. As long as the salary of a teacher in a parish school was determined by statute and calculated according to the value of a chalder, however, no real improvement was possible without a change in the law indeed, it meant that there was always the possibility of a decrease. With the land-owning classes still in the majority in Parliament even after the 1832 Reform Act, heritors were unlikely to vote for a change that would mean increased outlays for them. The legislation which had made heritors responsible for the salaries of parish schoolmasters and which doubtless had once protected the teachers' livelihood, had now become an impediment in their struggle for a better standard of living. Under the Highland Schools Act (1838) the Government had proposed to pay teachers not less than £22 which was taken as the minimum allowance for parish schoolmasters. According to the returns from presbyteries in 1841 salaries ranged from £25 to £34 with variable school fees. HMI John Gordon reported to the Committee of Council in 1844 that the average income across 1,557 schools was only about £19. In the burghs where salaries were met by the town council and where the 1803 Act was held not to apply, teachers were sometimes better off but the opposite could also be the case and councils would pay even less than the statutory amount. In Highland parishes and in the industrial Lowlands where many parents could not afford to pay much in the way of fees, a benefactor or a Kirk Session might pay the fees for them. One presbytery drew attention to an innovative practice in a mining area where the owner of a pit deducted from the wages of the men a sum sufficient to defray the school-fees for their children. On the whole teachers in rural schools had only the basic salary to live on.

While supporting the cause of parish schoolmasters the Education Committee found it difficult to increase the salaries of its own teachers. At this time the Church was still paying its teachers between £20 and £25 and most of them were appointed to situations where the fees, if any, were small. Poor salaries and conditions were a deterrent to the recruitment of well qualified teachers. Often teachers trained by the Church spent only a few years in an Assembly school before seeking more lucrative posts as parish or burgh school teachers. This meant that the Education Committee had to take teachers out of training after only six months or so to fill these recurring vacancies. Church of Scotland ministers must have been very much aware of how low teachers' salaries were compared to their stipends. For example in the small Dumfries-shire parish of Penpont with a population in 1831 of some 1,232 persons the minister's stipend was £210 while the emoluments of one of the two parish schoolmasters came to £45, a salary of £29 and fees of £16. The other teacher there received a salary of £22 and fees of £9. In Sanquhar where the minister's stipend was over £300 the teacher received a salary of £34 and fees came to only £15. Even in a grammar school the difference between the minister's stipend and the teacher's salary was considerable. In the town of Kirkcudbright with a population of 2,697, the average stipend of the ministers was £280, but in the grammar school a teacher received only £50 in salary and £60 in fees. Consequently in 1844 the General Assembly supported a petition drawn up by the parish schoolmasters in which it was submitted that instead of oatmeal, the salary should be fixed solely in money, and that the minimum be £40 and the maximum £50. In an attempt to strengthen their position and further their cause many schoolmasters took the matter into their own hands. In 1847 they formed themselves into the Educational Institute of Scotland with the aim of certifying the qualifications of teachers and thus improving their professional standing.

In an attempt to tackle the problem of schoolmasters' salaries at national level the Committee of Council drew up new regulations which were put into effect in 1848. These stated that teachers would be granted a sum of money from the Government equivalent to what they were being paid from voluntary subscriptions or local funds. Moreover, schoolmasters who took on apprentices or pupil teachers (sometimes called monitors) to be trained in teaching skills, would be paid an augmentation for the time spent in tutoring. These apprentice teachers (boys and girls often under thirteen years of age) would be paid a salary by the state ranging from £10 at the end of the first year to £20 at the end of five years, provided they passed an annual examination set by the inspectors. At the end of their apprenticeship in school they could win a Queen's scholarship and go on to a Normal school. Those who gained a Certificate of Merit at a Normal school would have their salary as teachers augmented by the Government. Schools where teachers were in receipt of any Government funding had always to be open to inspection, this included the inspection of religious instruction. It was laid down, moreover, that to qualify for any augmentation of salary schoolmasters had to forego the perquisites they received from undertaking other jobs. In Scotland the job of Session Clerk was exempt and in small parishes that of clerk to the heritors. Finally the Committee of Council was particular about the size of the schoolmaster's house and laid down that it had to have at least four rooms.

Perhaps the biggest stumbling-block to the implementation of the new scheme in Scotland was the Committee of Council's interpretation of the funds provided by the heritors. According to the Committee of Council because heritors were legally bound to pay schoolmasters' salaries, these could not be regarded as voluntary contributions and so schoolmasters paid in this way could not qualify for the proportional addition under the new arrangement. The Government's augmentation of salaries would only apply to any increase above the legal minimum (£25–£35) which heritors might choose to make. Heritors would also have to ensure that the size of the house provided met with the Committee of Council's regulations. For their part schoolmasters had to decide whether it was worthwhile relinquishing the perquisites on which many had depended to supplement their income. Once again government legislation drawn up to meet a national problem failed to take account of the Scottish situation. It proved impossible for schoolmasters in the Highlands to raise additional contributions either from fees or from heritors which would take their salaries above the legal minimum and so allow them to claim the government augmentation. When it came to Assembly Schools only in those cases where the salary paid by the committee was no more than £20, could teachers apply for a proportional amount of aid from the public purse. This was a derisory upper figure to propose. It would rule out most schoolmasters paid by the Church and those who could apply would have to relinquish all perquisites. The Government's proposals divided the Kirk. Many thought it wrong to agree to legislation which could benefit some Assembly schoolmasters but leave the parish schoolmasters no better off. In the end the Education Committee and the Assembly agreed accept the Government's scheme while regretting that it had really done nothing to assist most parish schoolteachers in Scotland. Angry at this decision Muir, the convener of the committee, resigned and would not be persuaded to change his mind. Earlier he had warned the Church of the risk that "inspection may advance to interference and interference, under the guidance of the hand that aids, may proceed to a control which shall at last shape both the matter of instruction and its form." And this, in his opinion, was exactly what the Church had done. While the General Assembly had voted against Muir's position it nevertheless took some cognizance of his fears and decided to present to the Privy Council and both Houses of Parliament a declaration safeguarding the Church's statutory right of superintendence of all schools while allowing for the right of the government to inspect those parish schools in receipt of government funding. These sentiments were embodied in the Acts of Assembly in the form of a *Protest, Declaration, and Testimony, on the subject of National Education.*

IDENTIFYING A NATIONAL SYSTEM
OF EDUCATION IN SCOTLAND

No matter how much the Church might protest and attempt to defend its statutory rights, it was evident that the more it became financially dependent on state funding, the more its control over school education was gradually eroded. Its financial dependence on the Council and the concessions it had made over the years meant that it had in reality lost control of school education and left it exposed to moves already underway for the introduction of a system under national or local government authority. In 1848 Lord Melgund, MP for Greenock, had written a pamphlet in support of a national system of education in Scotland and attacking the Privy Council's financial support of the education programmes run by the Established Church and the Free Church which he saw as in competition. The Committee of Council's policy, he maintained, only fostered sectarianism. Melgund believed that in Scotland unlike in England, a national system already existed in all but name. In his view all that was needed was to abolish the Established Church's traditional jurisdiction and superintendence of parish schools. He did concede that the Established Church had sought to advance the cause of education for the general good rather than for her own sectarian aggrandizement and he had to acknowledge that for the Education Committee "godly upbringing" had always meant not just religious instruction but included offering an all-round education which would prepare young people for life and work in the community.[6] Melgund was confident that his ideas had the support of dissenting bodies such as the United Presbyterian Church and that the Free Church would go along with him so long as religious instruction could be secured. Free Church men like James Begg had always held that the promotion of secular education was not one of the main duties of the church rather that it was the duty of the government to provide at least elementary education. In face of growing opposition both from other denominations and in political circles the Church continued to argue that its responsibility for the religious and educational interests of the nation and for a system of education based upon the Godly upbringing of youth was guaranteed by the Revolution Settlement and the Treaty of Union. The 1849 *Declaration*

6. In 1843 the Education Committee reported to the Assembly that over the previous five years among the 715 pupils who had left school to take up employment there were land-surveyors, civil engineers, overseers, road contractors, shipmasters, clerks in banks and counting-houses, and 180 schoolmasters.

and Protest, however, bore all the hallmarks of an Established Church with its back to the wall.

The debate in the 1849 General Assembly at which the convener had resigned had demonstrated a divided Church. Whereas some considered that that the Church's chief objective should be to adopt a strategy which would ensure a more adequate provision of schools and higher standards of education, many in the Church were more interested in defending a system of education which could be used first and foremost as a channel whereby the church could demonstrate its authority and as a bulwark of the Protestant faith. One manifestation of this division was the attitude to the growing number of Irish Catholic immigrants following the famine of 1846. By 1851 just over 7 percent of the Scottish population were Irish-born. This meant a corresponding rise in the number of Catholic schools. Some in the Church saw this as a threat to Protestantism and to the parish and Assembly schools which upheld the teaching of the Westminster Confession of Faith. The Education Committee itself was always anxious to promote the idea of the inclusion of children of all denominations in its own schools and in parish schools. In the interests of a good education it agreed, though sometimes reluctantly, to the Government's terms when it came to introducing school inspection or new ways of funding teacher training colleges. It regarded such state intervention, not as something to be regretted but as a positive step forward and as a way of building on what had already achieved. This said, the Education Committee did have reason to feel aggrieved and to sympathize with the Assembly's protestations. It may well have felt that the peculiarly Scottish national system of education which, with all its faults and deficiencies, had been in existence since the legislation of the seventeenth century, was in danger of being gradually undermined by a Privy Council which was bent on bringing English schools under government control and which for the last decade had been reluctant to acknowledge the uniqueness of the Scottish system. The Privy Council in applying its regulations for inspections and grants to Scotland was imposing these on a parish school system which had no equivalent in England. There was always the underlying feeling on the part of many in the Church that the legislators in London never really understood the school set-up in Scotland whether that be the way schoolmasters were paid or the time teachers were to spend in training. Whereas in Scotland parish schools and the authority of the Church of Scotland had been established by Acts of the Scottish Parliament and by the Act of Union, in England parish schools by and large were Church schools not regulated by statute. In a sense Scotland could claim to have had a unified national system of education going back to the seventeenth century in a way England could not. Moreover, there were significant differences in the standard of the education delivered. In Scotland elementary education was not seen as just for the poor. It had long been the tradition that the sons of the gentry attended the same schools as the sons (and daughters) of the poor, and it had been the ideal of the Reformers that all who were able should be given the chance of a university education. The curriculum in many parish and Assembly schools was not limited to teaching the three Rs but included Latin and Greek so that it was at least possible for the village school to prepare a boy for university. This was a system, therefore, which required teachers themselves to be well-educated and many were university graduates. Guaranteed a basic income and accommodation by law, the Scottish schoolmaster had a professional status not shared by his counterpart in England. All this explains why the Church of Scotland's Education Committee saw the system of pupil-teachers as likely to dilute the standards of Scottish teachers. It is also why the committee protested so vehemently when the Privy Council refused to recognize the fact that schoolmasters in Scotland could leave Normal schools after only a few months and still be well equipped to teach.

It would appear that at this point in time many in the Church failed, or refused, to appreciate the strength of the opposition and the growing popularity for moving towards some form of national system of education not under its supervision. The Educational Institute of Scotland, set up in 1847, was recruiting more and more teachers who wanted the opportunity to articulate their vision of a national system of education with improvements in salary and a high standard of professional training. Much of what the EIS stood for the Church of Scotland's Education Committee had been striving to attain since its inception. Further, for the most part many of the Government's principle educational aims were shared by the committee. Greater co-operation all round would have been to the benefit of education as a whole but the Church's fear of losing its prestige and authority damaged relationships and the Church became defensive rather than forward-looking. Joint initiatives of any kind were viewed with suspicion. In 1850 Melgund decided to put his proposals to the test in Parliament and in 1850 produced his School Establishment (Scotland) Bill, (A Bill to Reform and Extend the School Establishment of Scotland) and the battle for the Kirk's control of school education entered its final phase.

4

The Call for Reform

THE ARGUMENT FOR CHANGE

A S FAR AS SCHOOLING in Scotland was concerned the years from 1850 to the passing of the Education (Scotland) Act 1872 were dominated by the debate on national education. 1850 saw the first of a series of Bills considered by Parliament, all proposing changes to the Scottish education system and, in particular, that powers traditionally held by the heritors and the Established Church should be transferred to locally elected boards. Within the churches criticism of the existing system of school education came mainly from those connected with the recently formed United Presbyterian Church[1] and the Free Church of Scotland although when it came to proposing a solution, the latter denomination was not always of one mind. Critics were often scathing in their condemnation of the part played by the Established Church. In the opinion of Robert Candlish, convener of the Free Church Education Committee, parish schools were in the hands of a corrupt religious establishment, while Lord Advocate James Moncreiff, a Free Church elder and the presenter of a number of education bills in the 1850s, was convinced that the whole system needed reforming. Many of those who objected to the existing scheme maintained that the denominational system, whereby the different churches were allocated funds by the government, was divisive and that it should be replaced by a national government-supported system of parish schools managed locally and not answerable to any one denomination. Those who argued for changes to the system of Scottish education

---

1. The United Secession Church and the Relief Church united in 1847 to form the United Presbyterian Church.

were agreed on a number of main points. These were: that the existing means of education in Scotland were inadequate to meet current needs largely due to the deficiencies of the parish school system; that something had to be done to improve the lot of schoolmasters; that the expansion of education was one way of dealing with the rising crime rate and increasing immorality, particularly in the densely populated urban areas; and finally, that the Established Church's statutory monopoly with regard to the supervision of parish schools had to be abolished.

In many ways the shortcomings of the Established Church left it open to criticism. In the 1850s the inefficiency of presbyteries in their superintendence of schools and the ineffectiveness of these visits were frequently raised by its opponents and used as reasons for insisting on the need for change. Critics pointed to schools that had not been visited by a presbytery for many years. Thomas Guthrie, who had gone over to the Free Church in 1843, looking back on his ministry in the rural parish of Arbirlot before the Disruption, told a public meeting held in support of national education that although he had lived next door to the parish school for seven years he had no recollection of ever visiting it for the purpose of scrutinizing its efficiency except on that one day each year when the presbytery's committee came to examine it and even this examination was nothing but "a decent sham and the dreichest business I had ever to do." He claimed that hardly a single parish minister ever made it his business to supervise religious instruction and that all the talk about "godly upbringing" was "simply cant."[2] Further the Church was seen as powerless when it came to getting rid of bad teachers. Its statutory authority was much resented and the expectation that all parish schoolmasters would be members of the Church of Scotland was attacked as outmoded and limiting. The Established Church refuted these criticisms by producing annual reports which noted the regularity of presbytery visits and the detailed information submitted. In 1852, for example, some sixty-eight presbyteries (out of eighty-three) transmitted returns showing that 2,330 schools had been examined. These returns normally contained full accounts of the efficiency of the teacher, the standard of the accommodation, the attendance record of the pupils and the curriculum being covered. Attention was drawn to whatever was unsatisfactory particularly

---

2. Guthrie, *Report of the Proceedings at the Public Meeting of the Friends of National Education* 63 and 92. Guthrie was minister of Arbirlot Parish in Angus between 1827 and 1837.

where the buildings or the accommodation failed to meet government requirements. Sometimes thoughtful conclusions of a general nature accompanied the reports. In 1862, for example, the Presbytery of Ayr observed that for any system of education to be effective there would have to be some kind of legal requirement making school attendance compulsory. In addition to presbyterial superintendence, the secretary of the Education Committee continued to carry out routine visits to Assembly schools throughout the country in an endeavor to show that the Church took inspection seriously. It is difficult to assess what these examinations actually achieved, however, since neither the presbyteries nor the Education Committee ever gave accounts of action taken following the reports submitted.

Those agitating for reform made much of the number of children not attending school and this was often linked to expressions of concern for the immoral state of the nation. W. M. Hetherington, minister of Free St. Paul's, Edinburgh and editor of the *Free Church Magazine*, calculated in 1850 that 500,000 children were not provided for by parish schools and, even taking into account all the additional schools that were not parish schools, there still remained at least 200,000 children, between the ages of six and fifteen for whom there were no means of education, public or private. According to Hetherington, this was the root cause of what he described as "the rapidly advancing tide of intemperance, immorality and crime . . . and the increasing instances of juvenile depravity which fill our police and prison reports."[3]

That more schools were needed was never disputed by the Kirk, but it maintained that the irregular attendance of pupils was just as big a problem. In 1850 the Education Committee had conducted its own inquiry and had concluded that there were many poor and destitute children in the large towns who did not take advantage of the schooling that was available and many who left school at an early age to earn a wage. Even the Established Church's opponents had to concede that attendance at school was not a reliable way of estimating educational provision since many parents sent their children out to work in the factories to eke out the family income instead of sending them to school. The early Factory Acts (1833 and 1844) which ensured that children below thirteen attended school for not less than two hours a day, applied only to the textile mills. In many of

---

3. Hetherington, *National Education in Scotland viewed in Its Present Condition, Its Principles, and Its Possibilities*, 5.

the rural areas in Scotland children of agricultural workers only attended school in the winter. For the rest of the year children from nine years old were out in the fields earning their keep. It is questionable whether the reorganization of the parish school system would have solved this problem. Only legislation making full-time education compulsory would have helped. A number of years later, in 1863, with the introduction of the Revised Code[4] pending, the Education Committee made the keeping of attendance registers compulsory for all Assembly schools. It adopted the position that children who attended school less than 100 days throughout the year should not be included in any calculation of children receiving education.

How far the social and moral problems of this time could be laid at the door of the inadequate provision of school education is difficult to determine. Over and above juvenile crime many of the issues which concerned the Church related to adult behavior and to the changing lifestyles which accompanied the fast growth of urban areas. Intemperance, sexual promiscuity, inadequate housing, and poverty could hardly all be blamed on an inefficient education system. It was estimated that in just over twenty years the annual commitments for serious crime in Scotland had risen from about 1,800 to nearly 5,000 as a result of drunkenness. In 1850 the *Scotsman* newspaper describing Scotland's drink culture, commented with biting sarcasm: "It may seem strange that Edinburgh, the headquarters of the various sections of a clergy more powerful than any other save that of Ireland, should, in respect of drunkenness, exhibit scenes and habits unparalleled in any other metropolis, and that Glasgow, where the clergy swarm, should be notoriously the most guilty and offensive city in Christendom."[5]

There were those who believed that the answer to the immorality of the times lay in the growth of Sunday schools. Around the mid-1850's the Education Committee began including in its reports to the General Assembly the number of children attending Sunday schools who had not been attending the weekday schools. These were Sunday schools which supplemented the school education programme and taught basic subjects like reading and writing to children who were working on weekdays. In

4. The Revised Code proposed basing grants on numbers attending school for at least 176 days per annum, and on the attainment of certain standards in the three *R*s. See later section.

5. *Scotsman* in 1850. Quoted in Devine, *The Scottish Nation*, 350–51.

1849 the Edinburgh Sabbath School Teachers' Association submitted a report to the Education Committee stating that it had twenty-seven schools attended by 2,215 children and staffed by 229 teachers under its superintendence. It is likely, however, that these figures refer to Sunday schools under the supervision of local congregations whose main objects were evangelical outreach and missionary rather than educational. Whereas earlier Sunday schools had been established to fulfill both an educational and an evangelical purpose, with the passing of the Factory Acts and the possibility of children attending schools at least on a half-day basis on weekdays, there was less need for missionary-motivated Sunday schools to provide instruction in reading and writing. C. G. Brown has noted that by 1865, the Glasgow Sabbath School Union claimed that there was not a single affiliated Sunday school providing reading and writing at normal meetings. Between 1820 and 1870, Sunday schools had gradually lost their role as educational establishments and had become more rigorously religious institutions. Nevertheless both educational and evangelical Sunday schools could claim that, in their own way, they tackled the problem of immorality and crime.

One other matter which has to be considered under the heading of social and moral issues was the increasingly sectarian attitude to Roman Catholics.[6] The main Presbyterian Churches saw the increasing numbers of Roman Catholics as a threat to the Protestant tradition in Scotland and as a challenge to the prevailing system of school education. In the 1850s there was hardly a Presbytery in the land which did not have something to say about the dangers of "Papism." Fears were expressed that children might be influenced by books issued to schools by the Privy Council which were of a decidedly Catholic character containing passages which the Church of Scotland from its point of view regarded as historically false. While both the parish schools and the denominational schools in Scotland had a long history of inclusiveness, it would appear that the growing strength of the Catholic Church made the main denominations even more determined to ensure that, whatever the outcome of

---

6. There also seems to have been considerable opposition to Jews holding positions of authority. In 1848 and again in 1853 Perth Presbytery agreed to petition Parliament against Bills for the admission of Jews to seats in Parliament. James Bryce (*Public Education in relation to Scotland and its Parish Schools*, 2) claimed that following the passing of the Universities Test Act (1853), there was now no statutory obstacle to these chairs being filled by Jews, Papists, or Infidels.

the national education debate, Scottish schools would be Presbyterian schools and that teaching from the Authorized Version of the Bible and the Shorter Catechism would continue to be the main thrust of religious instruction. Such a dogmatic attitude was obviously resented by the Roman Catholic Church which now felt itself strong enough to make its voice heard and with the growth of Catholic schools, there was pressure on Catholic parents to send their children to their own church schools. A letter written by Bishop James Gillis to the Lord Provost of Edinburgh in 1854 made the Roman Catholic position clear with regard to school education: "We never can, and never will send our children to a school of which the master is not a Catholic, approved by his Bishop, or by those representing his Bishop's spiritual authority; and in which secular, as well as religious instruction, is not imparted to the scholars in the unmistake-able and untrammeled spirit of Catholic teaching . . . History never can be taught fairly to a Catholic child by a Protestant teacher; for the very documents that go to establish the hereditary claims of the pupil, would throw the master out of court."[7] Here were clear indications of how difficult it would be to include Roman Catholic schools in the kind of national system of education which those agitating for reform were now proposing.

ADVOCATES FOR CHANGE

The National Education Association's Proposals

Founded in 1850, the National Education Association of Scotland was set up with a view to supporting a national system of education. Like the churches it too was concerned about the increasing intemperance and crime in Scottish society and was critical of the way religious education was being delivered in parish schools. The High School in Edinburgh was held up as an example of what could be achieved. There a board of patrons comprised men of all sects and parties and the teachers belonged to all denominations. In common with others who argued for change the Association started from the premise that the existing system was sectarian being under the supervision of the Established Church. It was also highly critical of how teachers were selected and the amount they were paid by the heritors. It believed that state-funded education should be made available freely to everyone. In place of the heritors and presbyter-

7. Gillis, *A Letter to the Rt. Hon. Duncan Maclaren*, 6 and 12.

ies of the Established Church, it proposed that local boards should be elected by the male heads of families. These boards would appoint teachers, determine the curriculum, and manage the schools. The local boards would be supervised nationally by a central board. Teachers would not be required to subscribe to any religious test, and religious instruction, over which the government would have no control, would be determined by parents and the local boards.

The Position of the Free Church of Scotland

Within the Free Church of Scotland there was agreement that the Established Church's monopoly with regard to the appointment of teachers to parish schools had to be broken. Beyond that there were a number of divergent views as to how the education question should be tackled. Leading churchmen like Begg and Guthrie believed that having left the Established Church at the Disruption on the principle that there should be no state interference in ecclesiastical matters, the Church should not be dependent on state funding for its schools and training colleges. Begg denounced the existing Government scheme where even Catholic schools were subsidized. On the other hand he agreed that no denomination, not even the Free Church, was in a position to finance enough schools to meet the nation's needs. Begg favored a government funded scheme of national education within which the Free Church and the Established Church would co-operate in delivering religious education based on the Bible and the Shorter Catechism. For Begg the provision of secular education was the duty of the civil government while religious instruction should be the responsibility of parents and the church. His opponents, however, were not convinced that any national system would secure the desired scheme of religious instruction. Led by Robert Candlish the majority of ministers in the Free Church believed that they should press ahead with raising the necessary finance for the Free Church's own school education scheme. Fear of what effects a national system might have on the Free Church's schools made others similarly cautious of any proposal to completely dismantle the existing parish school system bad as it might be. Candlish, ever the astute political churchman who kept his own counsel, while opposing Begg and advocating the advantages of the Church's schools, was at the same time pursuing his own vision of what a national system might look like. In 1850 he wrote to the Marquis of

Lansdowne proposing that instead of parish teachers having to be members of the Established Church, all that should be required was that they should be Presbyterians. He favored a system whereby teachers would be appointed by householders and heads of families with all the Presbyterian churches having a right of periodical visitation and inspection but with a Central Board having the overall control of schools. Soon afterwards a group of Free Church ministers and elders, among them Hetherington, Cunningham, Candlish and A. E. Monteith, Sheriff of Fife, wrote to the Committee of Council on Education in similar terms. These proposals, however, did not go far enough to bring about any reconciliation with Begg and Guthrie and their supporters in the Free Church

The Position of the United Presbyterian Church of Scotland

The United Presbyterian Church took an approach which was even more radical than that of the Free Church in believing that the whole system, whereby the Government through the Committee of Council gave grants to the different denominations to run their schools, perpetuated sectarian animosity and even threatened civil liberty. Further it parted company with the majority in the Free Church in holding that the provision of religious instruction for young people did not fall within the province of the civil government but belonged exclusively to parents and the church. It was in favor of placing the management of schools under local boards, but disagreed with any attempt to legislate for religious instruction as part of the school curriculum even although it might be taught at certain stated hours or at the end of the school day and at a time when parents could withdraw their children.

By the mid 1850s, therefore, in all but those closely associated with the Established Church, there were hopes of changes to Scottish school education and, even where there was disagreement about how provision should be made for religious instruction, there was the desire that some form of national system would replace the Kirk's statutory hold on parish schools.

TOWARDS A NATIONAL SYSTEM OF SCHOOL EDUCATION IN SCOTLAND

From 1850 to the passing of the Parochial and Burgh Schoolmasters (Scotland) Act in 1861 five Bills to reform and extend school education in Scotland were brought to Parliament. All started from the claim that the means of education in Scotland were inadequate to cope with the growing population and its concentration in the Central belt, and set out to supplement the parish schools. All were in agreement that whereas the Established Church had statutory powers to examine parish schools, now some form of national system should bring these schools under the superintendence and inspection of a National Board with parish committees consisting of ministers, heritors, and householders or heads of families, taking responsibility for the management of existing schools and the establishment of new ones. All proposed that education should be paid for partly out of local taxes and partly by the Treasury. Likewise the law whereby only members of the Established Church could be schoolmasters was to be repealed and schoolmasters would no longer be required to subscribe to any declaration of faith. Over the years the various Bills differed mainly in the proposed constituency of the Central Board and in the concessions made to the various denominations particularly with regard to the delivery of religious instruction. From 1854 onwards the Bills also attempted to secure a higher salary for schoolmasters.

Viscount Melgund's Bills (1850 and 1851)

Viscount Melgund, the Liberal MP for Greenock, was the first to bring before Parliament proposals along the lines of those noted above. He suggested that a General Board of eleven people should be chosen to supervise all the parish schools in Scotland. The Parish Committee comprising the minister, the heritors and representatives of the General Board, would have powers to buy land and build schools, appoint and supervise all schoolmasters, and to fix the curriculum and the fees. There would be no faith requirement for schoolmasters. The funding of school education had to be met half by the committee locally and half by the Treasury. Melgund's proposals thus left considerable powers with parish ministers and local heritors. One section of the Bill actually stated that in parishes where a parish committee had not been established, the minister and heritors would continue to appoint the schoolmaster and superintend the parish schools. This Bill and another very similar one brought forward by him in 1851 were both rejected by the Commons, the latter losing by only thirteen votes.

Moncreiff's Bills (1854–1862)

Recognizing that the support for change was not going to go away in November 1853 the Church set up a special sub-committee to canvass the support of MPs and the Scottish landed class whose votes in Parliament would count in any division. A declaration backing the Church's position was signed by over 200 heritors and Justices of the Peace. As it happened in 1854, just as the General Assembly was congratulating itself on the defeat of Melgund's Bill, the push for a national system was taken up by the Lord Advocate James Moncreiff, MP for Leith, and was to become his great passion for the next ten years. Encouraged by the passing of his Bill to remove the religious test for university professors (except for appointments to theological chairs), Moncreiff pressed on with proposals to reform school education.[8] His Bills incorporated the general pattern of reform which had been proposed by Melgund, including the proposal to abolish the confessional test for schoolmasters, but with certain important changes by which he hoped he might achieve some kind of consensus among the Presbyterian churches. Whereas Melgund's Bills had made no clear statement regarding the teaching of religious instruction, the Preamble to the 1854 Bill showed a determination to secure its traditional place in the curriculum and revealed a strong Free Church influence. Moncreiff strongly believed that the majority of the Scottish people still wanted religious instruction to be taught as it always had been but that the Established Church's system of management, which he described in his Bill as "greatly defective," had singularly failed to meet the educational needs of the country. It was Moncreiff's intention that, while dismantling the existing system of supervision by the Established Church, religious instruction would be provided and taught by schoolmasters whose fitness would be examined by inspectors appointed by a Board of Education. His concession to the secular lobby and the United Presbyterian Church Synod was that religious instruction while forming part of the ordinary teaching of the school, would be offered at certain stated hours so that Catholic and Dissenting parents who objected to what was being taught could opt out. The make-up of the Board of Education now included the current president of the Educational Institute of Scotland and was heavily

8. The Universities (Scotland) Act was passed in 1853 by a majority of 106 votes to 17. It was agreed that every professor would make a declaration that he would not teach any doctrine opposed to the divine authority of the Bible or to the Westminster Confession.

weighted in favor of government officials. The abolition of the religious test meant that schoolmasters might be of any Protestant denomination but, as a concession to the Established Church, Moncreiff left the election of schoolmasters with the minister and heritors of the parish, their fitness having first been approved by the district inspector. Further the general day-to-day management of the existing parish schools would be left in the hands of heritors and parish ministers. New schools would be managed by Town Councils within the burghs and in rural areas by ratepayers. All schools would be under the over-all supervision of the national Board of Education. Educational Districts were to be set up with inspectors for each district. The new schools established by local committees were to be designated as "public schools" and the public schoolmaster could be dismissed by the Board of Education with or without notice and without any reason. Moncreiff's Bill would have guaranteed schoolmasters a minimum salary of £50, abolishing the traditional system whereby salaries had been fixed according to grain prices. Of this £50, heritors would continue to pay £34 and the remainder would be made up by the Privy Council. To make it possible for schoolmasters to retire owing to age or illness a retiring allowance of £25 was to be paid, half by the heritors and half by the Privy Council. As another concession to the churches Moncreiff would have made it lawful for the Board to grant aid to "Industrial or Reformatory" schools which would "help to cleanse out the fountainhead of crime . . . and convert the Arabs and Pariahs of our great towns into good and useful citizens." He even recommended that grants be given to Denominational Schools in poor localities provided the inspector reported these to be efficient and deserving and open to children of all denominations. Moncreiff proposed raising the money for this scheme by a property tax of a penny in the pound. This Bill was lost by only nine votes, with thirty-six Scottish MP's voting for it and fourteen against it.

Although his Bill to reform the Scottish educational system had been defeated, Moncreiff pressed on with his aim of achieving a greater financial stability for schoolmasters and in June 1854 he persuaded the Government to pass an Act guaranteeing that salaries of parish schoolmasters would be held for another year at the level fixed in 1828. Had they been calculated according to the 1854 price of grain the maximum salary would have fallen from £34 to £25 and the minimum from £25 to £19. These figures were looked at again in 1857 when it was agreed that

Sheriffs and Stewards should make a new calculation which would be applied as from 1859. This would secure for schoolmasters a salary fixed for twenty-five years based on the average price of a chalder of oatmeal in 1859.

Recognizing that his previous education bill had only narrowly been defeated in March 1854, the Lord Advocate did not give up. In July 1855 and again in 1856 he laid another two Bills before parliament. To try and placate the Established Church he withdrew from the preamble to his 1855 Bill the description of the parish schools as being greatly defective. Responding to the ill-feeling created by his previous proposal that public schoolmasters could be dismissed without reasons being given and without the chance to appeal, Moncreiff now proposed that the Board could only dismiss them after due inquiry had been made. Schools committees were to have powers to appoint female assistant teachers and to separate male and female pupils into different classes as they saw fit and, in response to criticisms from the secular lobby, the suggestion that the Board might aid some denominational schools was dropped. These Bills suffered the same fate as his previous one and for the same reasons. While Moncreiff had had the support of the Scottish burghs and the Liberal middle-class—for example, a petition of the merchants, bankers, solicitors, surgeons, and traders, in Peterhead had supported the Bill but asked that religious instruction should be of an entirely non-controversial character and acceptable to all denominations—there can be little doubt that events in England were making Moncreiff's task more difficult. It could be said these were Scottish bills defeated by an English vote, with English dissenters, Conservative MP's, and Roman Catholics all voting against them. In 1854 he had expressed his anger at the disinterest of some eighty or ninety English MPs, resident in London, who had been absent from the Commons when the division was put. Years later he admitted that the English members had been afraid that the passing of this Bill might have encouraged those advocating changes in England to step up their efforts. During 1855 three Bills had been brought forward in an attempt to promote the establishment of new schools in England outwith the control of the Church of England. All three failed but the attempts must have alarmed the English establishment where there was an even greater resistance to change. MPs south of the border who wanted to protect the Church of England's privileged position with regard to its schools, were not going to vote for a change to the Scottish system and so weaken their own case. It is no wonder that the National Association for the Vindication of Scottish Rights (formed in 1853) argued that Scottish interests were being neglected at Westminster. This Association was warmly supported by James Begg who believed that Scotland should have a greater say in its own government. Begg also gave his support to the newly formed Scottish Social Reform Association which campaigned for better housing and the reform of land laws. While the National Association for the Vindication of Scottish Rights was only active for three years, when taken together with the formation of the National Education Association of Scotland and the move for social reform we can identify early indications that in some quarters there was a stirring of feelings for Scottish nationalism.

The position of the Scottish heritors in all this is interesting. Generally speaking they supported the Established Church's position in opposing the proposed changes. Presumably any democratization would have diminished their power. On the other hand many of Moncreiff's proposals included provision for ratepayers being assessed for the upkeep of schools which could have meant a considerable financial saving for the heritors. Over a third of Assembly schoolmasters had their salaries augmented by heritors to enable them to claim government augmentation. Some of the heritors, however, were Episcopalians and there was no love lost between them and the Free Church and they opposed Moncreiff's Bills as expressions of Free Church Liberal politics. Their abhorrence of the Free Church was such that when in 1860 the Established Church had to appeal for money for its Committee for the Endowment of Chapels a letter of support was signed by some twenty of the Scottish nobility, eleven of whom were Episcopalians.

The Parochial and Burgh Schoolmasters Act (1861)

By 1860 it was apparent that James Moncreiff was not one to give in easily. Heartened by his success in steering the Parochial and Schoolmasters (Scotland) Act 1857 through Parliament, he decided to bring forward yet another Bill in an attempt to reform Scottish education. Described as James Moncreiff's most important single contribution to Scottish education, the 1861 Bill again contained measures which Moncreiff hoped would help to win over some of his adversaries in Scotland. He recognized, for example, that the poor salaries and conditions of schoolmasters had always been one of the Established Church's main concerns and that the solution proposed by the 1857 Act had not addressed the root cause of the problem. In his new Bill, therefore, he tackled this issue by putting forward an answer which Scottish schoolmasters had been advocating for many years, namely that salaries should be fixed at a certain rate independent of the price of oatmeal. Moncreiff proposed that salaries should be not less than £40 and not more than £60, the appropriate figure being agreed by the heritors and minister of the parish and payable according to the Valuation Roll one half by proprietors and one half by tenants or occupiers. An amendment to the Bill raised salaries to a minimum of £50 and a maximum of £80. The schoolmaster was to be able to retire on an allowance not exceeding two-thirds of his salary. As far as the choice of teachers was concerned the parish minister could still act with the heritors in the appointment but the examination of appointees was to be by four boards of examiners set up in connection with the universities thus removing this power from presbyteries. There was to be no test of faith or signing of a confession of faith, instead teachers would make the following declaration:

> I,—, do solemnly and sincerely in the presence of God profess, testify and declare that as schoolmaster of the parish school at—in the parish of —, and in discharge of the said office, I will never endeavour, directly or indirectly, to teach or inculcate any opinions opposed to the divine authority of the Holy Scriptures, or to the doctrines contained in the Shorter Catechism agreed upon by the Assembly of Divines at Westminster, and approved by the General Assembly of the Church of Scotland, in the year 1648; and that I will faithfully conform thereto in my teaching of the said school, and that I will not exercise the functions of the said office to the prejudice or subversion of the Church of Scotland as by law established, or the doctrines and privileges thereof.[9]

This latter measure was intended to placate those denominations jealous of the Established Church's powers to appoint as parish schoolmasters only those who accepted its doctrinal position and at the same time win the approval of all who wanted to retain the Protestant tradition. It would certainly not have pleased the Scottish Episcopalians, however, and was totally unacceptable to Roman Catholics.

---

9. Parliamentary Papers, Public Bills 1861 III 7 June 1861 24 Vict., and 12 July 1861 24 & 25 Vict.

In cases of complaint against schoolmasters the Bill transferred the disciplinary powers of the presbytery to the sheriff of the county although the minister and heritors or presbytery clerks could still make complaints in writing to the sheriff charging schoolmasters with immoral conduct or cruel treatment of pupils. Presbyteries still retained the right to fix the hours of teaching and the length of the vacation. Moreover where it could be shown that schoolmasters were neglecting their duties due to infirmity or old age, the heritors and minister, with the concurrence of HM Inspector and the presbytery, could require the schoolmaster to resign. Finally heritors and ministers were encouraged to appoint female teachers at salaries not above £30, to give instruction in "industrial and household training" as well as elementary education. In all of this the Church was still given a place in the management of schools and the right to make complaints about schoolmasters would have to entail some school visitations.

With these proposals the Lord Advocate believed he had done his best for the Kirk but clearly his main objective had been to find a compromise that suited all parties, particularly the other denominations. He even told the Commons that he had brought the Bill forward late in the session to give the General Assembly the opportunity to consider its terms but it is doubtful if this made any difference. The reaction of the Church was totally negative. It went through its usual routine of commending anything that would improve the lot of schoolmasters and condemning everything that threatened its own position. No matter how much time for discussion it would have been given the Church was never going to settle for anything less than a full restoration of its superintending powers. For his part Moncreiff, having heard the Established Church rehearse its position so often, had no intention of paying any heed to it and the Act received royal assent in August 1861.

In 1862 Moncreiff made one final attempt to introduce a national system of education into Scotland. If anything this latest—A Bill to make further provision for the Education of the People in Scotland—was perhaps his most radical. Over and above what had been achieved in the 1861 Act his intention now was to legislate for the establishment of additional parish schools in towns and in rural districts. The implementation of the Bill's proposals would have completely undermined all the Established Church's efforts to meet Scotland's educational needs. Indeed, it would have eventually eliminated all the Presbyterian denominational schools by cutting off existing government grants and there would have been no money for any new building apart from parish schools. Further the Bill made no attempt to secure a place for religious instruction in the curriculum and went so far as to remove entirely any requirement for a schoolmaster to make the declaration set out in the 1861 Act. The Assembly's Education Committee pointed out that this seemed to fly in the face of existing Privy Council regulations whereby no grant was given to any school where religious instruction was not taught. In spite of the crippling effect the Bill would have had on Assembly schools some members of the Church felt obliged to acknowledge its main aim which was to enlarge the parish school system and establish additional schools. At the Commission of Assembly which met in April 1862 a motion that the Assembly should not oppose the Bill went to a division but lost by sixteen votes to three. On this occasion the Established Church's opposition to Moncreiff's proposals was widely supported. Both Scottish and English MPs recognised the threat to religious education. Moncreiff eventually withdrew the Bill having concluded that "without full inquiry into the educational state of Scotland it was of no use to go on with this incessant knocking at the doors of Parliament." With this latter sentiment there was increasing support in Scotland and it is no coincidence that in April that year Paisley Presbytery sent up an overture calling on the Assembly to petition Parliament for a Royal Commission to inquire into the whole condition and wants of Education in Scotland, prior to any further legislation on the subject.

ASSEMBLY SCHOOLS 1850-63

A Time of Consolidation

While fending off these attempts to introduce a new national system of education took up much of the time and attention of the Education Committee, other aspects of its work were not neglected. During this period it consolidated its school education programme in various ways. Between 1849 and 1863 the number of Assembly schools actually fell from 208 to 195 (of which twenty-five were female schools) but in that same period the committee had branched out into industrial schools and had established sixty-three sewing schools. That more schools were not planted at this time was due to a number of factors. There was competition and opposition from other denominations particularly in the Highlands and Islands where the Free Church often built schools in close proximity to Established Church schools. In 1849 Robert Campbell, a teacher at Skerray in Sutherland, complained that as a result of the violent and personal exertions of the Free Church the people were afraid to send their children to his school, and suggested that the school should be closed. The Presbytery of Uist objected to the fact that the teachers of the Free Church attracted children to their schools by handing out biscuits, clothes, books, and stationery. The main reason for the Established Church not making further educational provision during this period, however, was its inability to raise sufficient funds so that the committee had a struggle to balance its books. The financial report in 1851 showing an Annual Expenditure of £6,400 and an Ordinary Income of £5,200, of which only about half came from congregational collections, was typical. The matter was not helped by the fact that up until 1853 it was still endeavoring to pay off the debt incurred in connection with the Glasgow Normal School buildings. In that year the committee reported to the General Assembly that its funds were exhausted. It noted that there were at least 150 places where schools were needed and where accommodation could be provided but where it could not afford to place a teacher. Often appeals had to be made for special purposes such as the development of agricultural instruction in the Highlands and the establishment of more female schools, industrial training for girls having become one of the Committee of Council's latest priorities. The committee informed the Assembly in 1862 that there had been a poor response to an appeal for donations towards setting up more female schools but that the situation had been saved by the liberality of Miss Burdett Coutts who undertook to fund seven sewing schools in connection with Assembly schools. The Bell Trustees helped the committee with the maintenance of twenty sewing schools and the Duke of Sutherland agreed to support five such schools on his estates. The Duke also made land available for agricultural instruction and offered to make the necessary provisions for the teaching of this subject at any suitable school in the County of Sutherland. Apart from the financing of these new developments, the Church had continually to consider the viability of existing schools. Where the uptake was low or where school buildings were in a poor state of repair, the Church had no alternative but to close them.

As for making better provision for its teachers, the Established Church found the Committee of Council's regulations a considerable impediment. In 1848 it had tried to persuade the Council to reverse its decision with regard to the conditions relating to government augmentation but having failed the matter was dropped. As a result Assembly schoolmasters were often unable to take advantage of the government's scheme and the Church lost some of its best teachers. The Council's secretary Kay-Shuttleworth calculated that the failure to meet the government's regulations had meant that in 1852 grants to schools in connection with the Established Church (presumably including parish schools) were about £1,350 less than those made to the Free Church and other schools. His solution was that the Established Church should make an effort to raise some £20,000 extra funding from the heritors and from voluntary subscriptions. Even to make such a suggestion showed how out of touch he was with the Scottish scene where for a long time the Established Church had been struggling to pay its teachers £25 per annum from these very contributions. While in some places heritors were willing to supplement schoolmasters' salaries, there were a number of situations particularly on the Islands where presbyteries seem to have been unable to persuade heritors to maintain or provide buildings which met the Committee of Council's requirements and so help schoolmasters qualify. In 1856 the Assembly was informed that many teachers leaving the Normal school with certificates did not go to Assembly schools but to places where there was a school building and schoolhouse accommodation which did meet Government requirements and so qualified for augmentation. Towards the close of this decade, however, most Assembly teachers had managed to raise their total emoluments one way or another, through augmentation or through fees or by taking on pupil teachers. By 1859 the average income of 112 teachers in Assembly Schools in the Highlands and Islands was about £50. In other parts of the country the average was over £63 while teachers in female schools could earn up to £33.

Where the Education Committee was itself unable to provide funding for schools it recognized the considerable contribution from local efforts and from private endowments such as the Dick and Milne Bequests from which several schools benefited. Increasingly schools were being established by local churches and by private individuals. In the parish of Carnock (a mining district in Fife), for example, the proprietors of the Forth Iron Works provided a school for their workers' families and appointed a headmaster with three assistants, one of whom was a female teacher for girls. In the parish of Dunotter the minister built a school at his own expense, and in the parish of Roberton (Selkirk) a school was set up by the Duke of Buccleuch. It was reckoned that by 1850 there were 104 Sessional schools in Scotland, many of them in Glasgow. Sometimes congregational collections for the national fund suffered as a result of such local efforts, however, and the committee's work was held up.

Learning and Teaching in Assembly Schools

The development of teacher training was the most encouraging sphere of the Education Committee's work at this time. As had been foreseen by Muir and others who had opposed the Church's financial agreement with the Committee of Council in 1849, as time passed the General Assembly's Education Committee found itself continually having to adapt to conditions laid down by that Council, but in many ways this proved to be no bad thing. The funding arrangement for Normal schools in Scotland was a case in point. In 1848 the Committee of Council had reluctantly agreed not to enforce its proposed new scheme in Scotland. By 1852, however, it had decided that certain changes relating to the salaries of teachers in Training schools and the supply of books for students, which had already been in operation in the rest of the United Kingdom, would then be applied to the Normal schools in Edinburgh and Glasgow. The proposals meant a reduction in the Council's annual grant with this loss being compensated by book grants and by per capita payments for each student according to the standard of the certificate received at the end of each year, an average of £25 for each student. In addition each year Queen's scholarships amounting to £45 or £50 would be awarded to a number of pupil-teachers (or apprentices) going on to Normal schools, on examination by HM Inspectors. Having calculated that this new plan would be to their financial advantage the committee agreed to these proposals and the following year it was able to report that with the number of students successfully obtaining government certificates its income for the management of Normal schools had risen considerably.

The Church had only begun to benefit from this new system of funding, however, when the Committee of Council proposed further changes. These involved the introduction of a three-year course for students with awards and grants increasing proportionally each year. Whereas the majority of students had normally attended for only one year, there was now a financial incentive to Normal schools to urge students to undertake longer courses. Moreover, the restriction on the intake of Queen's scholars, formerly one-fourth of the students in residence during the year, was lifted. This meant an increase in income from that source. Acknowledging that a longer period of instruction should mean better qualified teachers, the General Assembly accepted the Committee of Council's proposals, insisting only that Latin should remain a compulsory subject for apprentice teachers and for students being presented for Queen's scholarships. For the Church the down side of having better qualified teachers was that even more of them opted for better paid posts in parish schools rather than in Assembly schools. This situation pertained until 1863 when questions were raised by the Committee of Council on the number of Queen's Scholars being admitted to training colleges in Scotland.[10] It would appear that, having advised all those above the age of eighteen who wished to undertake teacher training to present themselves for Queen's Scholarships and sit the appropriate Privy Council examination, so many had been successful that the number attending Normal schools had risen above what the Committee of Council was prepared to support and it demanded that the Church should reduce its student numbers by ninety. This demand angered the committee. Having tried to work with the Committee of Council's strategy, it was now to be penalized. Part of the disagreement centered on the question of whether the supply of teachers was in excess of available posts. The outcome of the dispute was that the Committee of Council decided to alter the whole system and to do way with Queen's Scholarships altogether. Henceforth the Church would only receive government grants for those students who had qualified after two years training and had completed a two-year probationary period in an elementary school. The Education Committee saw these new funding provisions as a possible threat to the future of the Church's Normal schools since it would lose out on students who failed to complete the four-year training period.

The curriculum to be followed by teachers in training was extensive. Students were expected to be proficient in all branches of a liberal edu-

---

10. The term "training college" is first used in the 1862 Education Committee Report. For a number of years subsequently the terms "Training College" and "Normal School" seem to have been inter-changeable. "Model Schools" attached to Normal Schools for practical training in a classroom situation, became known as "Practicing Schools."

cation. This included School Management, the Theory and Practice of Education, as well as English, arithmetic, elementary geography (Great Britain and Palestine), general history, natural history, singing, religious knowledge, and at a later stage Latin, Greek, and mathematics. There was also a growing emphasis on practical subjects such as sewing, agriculture and drawing. It was discovered that not all students were fit to cover so many subjects so the committee decided that it would divide students into different classes, the lower class taking fewer subjects than the rest. Recognizing the usefulness of lessons in agriculture, the committee opened this subject to everyone. Some knowledge of agriculture was particularly useful to teachers taking up posts in rural areas where farming was the chief occupation. With the increasing emphasis on female education and skills in laundry and cooking, the committee decided in 1858 that there was sufficient money in the funds of the Edinburgh Normal School to allow it to purchase a large house to provide accommodation for female student teachers supervised by a matron. (The Scottish Ladies Association had already been running a boarding-house for female students from country districts since 1848.)

As for the curriculum in Assembly schools during this period, while religious instruction and the three Rs remained high on the agenda, with mathematics and Latin being offered in a considerable number of schools to a few of the pupils, there was also an emphasis on developing practical skills. In line with the training offered at the Normal schools we find an increasing number of female schools and sewing schools for women and agricultural and industrial schools for men. It was the view of the Education Committee that the latter held the key to opening up employment for young people and so improving the standard of living in the Highlands. During the 1850s it became the official government policy to promote instruction in what it described as "Industrial Occupations." The Census of 1851 recorded that in Scotland there were 50 boys' schools and 809 girls' schools teaching practical subjects.[11] In particular it was seen as important to educate girls to enable them to prepare them for looking after a family and running a home. The Committee of Council had put pressure on the Church by declaring that for the purposes of funding in mixed schools where there was no female teacher to instruct the girls in sewing and cutting, only the boys would be counted. The Education

11. See Appendix 4.1.

Committee estimated that by 1862 in landward parishes alone there were 800 or 900 separate female schools, and, in addition to this, 500 or 600 sewing departments.

If literacy is taken to include writing as well as reading ability, there seem to have been gaps here. Many were leaving school able to read but unable to write. Assembly statistics revealed that there were many pupils on the roll who did not attend a Writing class. In 1859 only 64 percent of pupils at Assembly schools were learning to write. In 1855 the Education Committee had persuaded the Committee of Council to retain some knowledge of Latin as compulsory for all pupil teachers entering a Normal school as a Queen's Scholar. In fact, while Latin may have been offered widely, the number of pupils actually taking it seems to have been very small, only about 1.5 percent compared to 5 percent in parish schools. Regulations issued by the Assembly in 1863 required schoolmasters to teach Music where it was practical to do so, and the basics of Drawing when this could be done without encroaching on the time needed for other compulsory subjects.

One notable feature of this time was the gap between the subjects teachers were trained in and the subjects actually taught in Church schools. The Rector's Report of the Glasgow Normal School in May 1850 recorded instruction being given in English (Reading, Grammar and Composition), Natural Science, Geography, History, Latin, Greek (not compulsory), Arithmetic, Mensuration, Mechanics, Geometry, Trigonometry, Algebra, Music, and Religious Instruction. When this very full curriculum is compared with what was actually being taught in many Assembly schools it is clear teachers were often too well qualified. It is no wonder many opted for parish schools. It would appear that the broad comprehensive curriculum covered in Normal schools in Scotland was out of step with what was expected of their counterparts in England. In a letter to the Committee of Council in 1854, Henry Moseley HM Inspector of Schools, had insisted that government grants to Normal schools were expressly for the promotion of elementary education. In his proposed curriculum, which he claimed was based on the principle of attempting a little and doing it well as opposed to the practice of attempting a great deal and doing it badly, there was no time set aside for languages such as French or Latin nor for practical subjects such as agriculture and female domestic skills.

THE REVISED CODE

As early as May 1859 the Education Committee had warned the Assembly that a system of capitation grants, based on the number of scholars attending school for a minimum of 176 days in the year, would be extended to Scotland the next year.[12] At that time it was the committee's view that the introduction of this system would be of considerable benefit to Scotland, particularly to the Highlands, since the allowance paid would not depend on the state of the buildings. Further as seven-tenths of the capitation grant was to be regarded as representing local voluntary contributions, more teachers would be able to claim the government augmentation. In February 1860, however, the committee received a letter from the Committee of Council explaining that as a Royal Commission of Inquiry into the state of education in England and Wales (the Newcastle Commission) was reviewing all forms of government funding, including capitation grants, it had been decided not to include Scotland in the estimate for capitation grants for the year 1860–1861. The Council also stated that it intended to ensure that there would be no distinction between one part of Great Britain and another in the distribution of grants. In 1861, the Vice-President of the Committee of Council, proposed a Revised Code for England and Wales. This would replace grants made for different purposes, salaries and pensions, school books, and apparatus, etc., with an annual grant to cover all expenditure payable to school managers and calculated on the attendance and performance of the pupils—this was payment by results. In its report in 1862 the Church's committee produced a comprehensive account of the proposed Revised Code and its implications for the funding of schools in Scotland. It concluded that, while objecting to many of the details of the Code, it would give support to its general principles in so far as it aimed at encouraging more regular attendance at school, promoting evening schools, throwing greater responsibility on school managers, and simplifying payments. The committee, nevertheless, were not slow to pick up on the discrepancy between the proposals of the Revised Code and those of Moncreiff's 1862 Bill and pointed out that the latter discontinued all grants to all but parish schools. As it turned out Moncreiff's Bill was withdrawn and the Revised Code was suspended for a year. In May 1863 the Education Committee was

12. Capitation grants had been introduced by the Committee of Council into schools in England in 1853.

in a position to announce to the General Assembly that the Code would take effect as from 30 June in the case of applications for grants for new schools and for Pupil-Teachers, and would be applied generally after 31 March 1864. In preparation for this the committee issued new guidelines and regulations for teachers outlining a new curriculum and, for the first time, making it compulsory to keep a register. It entered into negotiations with the Privy Council hoping to persuade it to restore the £5 additional grant for schools in Gaelic-speaking districts and to permit it to employ licentiates of the Church as teachers. Both requests were rejected. The Committee of Council advised the Church to employ mistresses rather than masters where schools in the Highlands were short of money. It also rather harshly reprimanded the committee for employing sewing-mistresses for the industrial instruction of girls instead of trained female teachers who might also help to teach elementary subjects. As it turned out the Revised Code did not apply in Scotland until May 1864 and operated fully for only six weeks, that is until 10 June, when the appointment of the Argyll Commission was announced, and payment by results was not introduced fully into Scotland until the Scotch Code of 1873.

THE KIRK'S RESPONSE TO CHANGE

Throughout the 1850s the Established Church remained firm in opposing the various attempts to reform the system of parish school education in Scotland. Whenever there was news of a forthcoming Bill the General Assembly or a Commission of Assembly would meet and immediately launch an attack on whatever was being proposed. At the same time, while there were no major divisions in the ranks, there were some who would have adopted a more conciliatory approach which recognized those instances where the proposals being considered coincided with the aims of the Church. For example there was support for Moncreiff's efforts to secure better conditions for schoolmasters. These had included some provision for retirement allowances. The majority accepted the Church's dependence on Privy Council funding and the more liberal minded, hoping no doubt that the Council would look upon them favorably, were even willing to recognize that other denominations also had a right to benefit from government funding, a position which was intended to counter the opposition's accusation that the Church's attitude was sectarian. There was a considerable minority, however, who saw this as the Church

sanctioning the endowment of all sects and abandoning the unique status of the Church of Scotland established by law. While noting that in
Moncreiff's earlier Bills the provision for religious instruction was not all
that they would have liked, some would have gone as far as to admit to
being grateful that the necessity of such instruction was being recognized.
Some of the elders of the Kirk were willing to give a cautious support to
what Moncreiff was attempting as long as the test for schoolmasters and
the superintendence of presbyteries were retained and there was a view
that the choice of parish schoolmasters should no longer be restricted to
those who belonged to the established Church. On the whole, however,
the majority in the Church were opposed to any move to introduce a
national system. Declarations defending the Established Church's traditional rights and authority as stated in 1849 were reiterated no matter what was proposed by those who sought to make changes. The Kirk
stubbornly held to its view that its authority and superintendence was
guaranteed by statute and that the place of religious instruction within
the school curriculum was of paramount importance and could only be
secured by insisting that schoolmasters must be members of the Kirk.
Moreover, while admitting that much still needed to be done to meet the
educational needs of Scotland's young people, the Church denied that the
existing provision was as deficient as its critics claimed and pointed to its
own contribution. It claimed, for example, that it had more than double
the number of schools than all the other denominations put together, that
more members of the Church contributed to school education, and that
it spent five times more on schools than was spent by the Free Church.

By 1854 when the results of the 1851 Census were made public, the
defenders of the Established Church believed that they could show that
Scottish school education was not nearly in as perilous a state as its critics had claimed. The Census had shown that, even allowing for incomplete statistics, (the inquiry in Scotland was a voluntary measure unlike
England) the proportion of the population at day schools was estimated
at 1 in 7 of the Scottish population. This figure was frequently quoted by
supporters of the Established Church as contradicting those who claimed
that the Scottish system was wholly deficient and it appeared even better when compared with the situation in England and Wales which was
reported as 1 in 13. Some went further and pointed out that even in the
remote parts of the Highlands and Islands 1 in 5 attended school at some
time of the year and that nothing in any of the proposed legislation would

benefit very much those living there. Indeed there was nothing that better paid and well-qualified teachers could not put right under the superintendence of presbyteries and subject to examination by government inspectors so why exchange some new untried system for a system that had proved so beneficial to the nation for over a hundred years?

One result of the proposals for a national education system over this period was that for many in the Church the "godly upbringing of youth" had to be secured at all costs and was in danger of becoming more important than the delivery of a broad curriculum. The Church continually left itself open to the charge that its schools were merely "Bible Schools." The various government Bills were accused of making no provision for ascertaining the religious character and faith of the teachers and no adequate superintendence of religious teaching. The Established Church maintained that to treat religious instruction in the way suggested by those who advocated removing it from the compulsory curriculum would create a secular system of education. To the accusation of secularism the Lord Advocate had this to say to his opponents in the Church: "How can there be any accurate distinction taken between Secular and Religious Instruction? For if by Secular we mean that which belongs to the present day, which is conversant with the things of daily life, which deals with daily duties, which relates to the services we owe to our families, to the community, and to the State, in short, our perpetual obligations to God and man, there is nothing more secular than religion."[13]

In holding to its principles as it did the Established Church exhibited towards the end of the 1850s a growing confidence in what it stood for and in what it was trying to achieve. This was a church which had entered into a new chapter in its history. The beginning of the recovery of the Established Church in the 1850s and 1860s has been described by a number of historians. T. M. Devine noted that "it [the Established Church] soon experienced something of a renewal under the leadership of men such as Norman Macleod of the Barony Church in Glasgow and James Robertson, Professor of Ecclesiastical History at Edinburgh. Their concern was to demonstrate that only an Established Church could be truly national and care for all the people."[14] The statistical evidence for this recovery has been offered by C. G. Brown who noted that by the

13. Speech of the Lord Advocate, 19–20.

14. Devine, *The Scottish Nation*, 378.

1860's the Church of Scotland was slowly regaining ground in attract-
ing members and adherents, accounting for 48 percent of Presbyterian
church members in contrast to the Free Church's 32 percent and the
United Presbyterian's 20 percent.

Unlike the late 1840's now the intransigence of the Established
Church when faced with legislation which threatened its status was no
longer an expression of anxiety at losing control and authority, but rather
the indication of a clear conviction in its God-given responsibility to defend the faith. It believed it was being true to itself and its historic principles in opposing Moncreiff's Bills. It had a genuine belief in the value of
the parish school system, what it had done and could do for Scotland, and
saw Moncreiff's proposals as undermining this. In the face of the growing
strength of the Roman Catholic Church and of a society perceived as becoming increasingly secularized, to weaken the Church's hold on schools
was to threaten Protestant beliefs and jeopardize the future of religious
instruction. There was much that was true and logical in the Established
Church's arguments. It was not the existence of the test taken by schoolmasters nor even the inadequate supervision of presbyteries that created
the shortage of schools or the poor attendance of the children, so why put
the blame on these? Moreover the Established Church could point out
that it was not alone in wanting to protect religious instruction since all
parties agreed that it was necessary for the moral welfare of the nation.
Again it would have been possible for the government to increase its aid
and give a fairer share to the educational programme of all denominations thus obviating the accusation that the existing system incited a sectarian spirit. What all the churches stopped short of admitting was that
no matter how many more schools they themselves tried to set up, there
was a limit to what the voluntary sector could accomplish and, even more
significantly, there was a limit to what could be expected of the heritors. A
parish school system which was territorial and which was dependent on
the co-operation and generosity of the landed class could no longer cope
with the situation as it had developed.

We have seen that on all sides throughout this controversy there
were signs of a willingness to accept change. Would a compromise solution have been possible? Moncreiff while pursuing his vision of a system
of national education saw that this could not be achieved without making
some concessions to the churches. By 1854 the Free Church's position
had progressed to the extent that, with some suggested amendments, its

General Assembly was happy to support the Lord Advocate's Bill. It would appear that there was a sizeable body within the Free Church, including that astute church politician Candlish, who were willing not only to reach some agreement with Moncreiff, but also to work alongside the Established Church had that Church been willing to surrender its monopoly on the oversight of parish schools. Begg, too, had visualized the possibility of the Free Church and the Established Church co-operating to secure religious instruction within a national system. One Scottish MP suggested that since almost all religious denominations in Scotland subscribed to the Westminster Confession, all that needed to be done was to alter the wording of that part of the test which referred to submitting to the discipline and authority *of this Church*, meaning the Established Church. Even within the Established Church's ranks there were those who recognized the positive aspects of Moncreiff's proposals. In spite of the fact that the Privy Council had kept changing its mind with regard to funding Normal schools the Kirk had demonstrated its willingness to go along with change as, for example, in the positive attitude it adopted to the proposed Revised Code. Moncreiff might have won more support from the Established Church had he been more courageous in pursuing the cause of the schoolmasters. It is disappointing that the Established Church, in its robust defense of its principles, should not have seen fit to explore further the implications of some of Moncreiff's earlier proposals. Like Lord Melgund before him the Bills he introduced in 1855 and 1856 left the minister and heritors with considerable powers to discipline and examine schoolmasters and presbyteries still retained the right to fix the hours of teaching and the length of the vacation. Had the Church entered into negotiations at this time it might have ended up in a stronger position than it did in 1861. Unfortunately the majority were not interested in making terms with either Moncreiff or the Free Church. Certainly after 1861 any agreement among the three Presbyterian Churches seemed as far off as ever. Moncreiff's 1862 Bill annoyed the United Presbyterians because it continued Privy Council grants to the Episcopalians and Roman Catholics. The Free Church believed that under the 1861 Act the Established Church had still too much influence and that in 1862 Moncreiff had framed his bill upon the principle of going as far as he could to conciliate the lairds and the Established Church.

Moncreiff's repeated attempts at reform may be seen as a kind of softening up process culminating in the 1861 Act. The interest he took in the welfare of the schoolmasters, the place he was initially willing to give to religious instruction and his show of favor towards the heritors, the Episcopalians and the Roman Catholics, all helped to win him support in different quarters, and yet, somewhat paradoxically, thwarted any possible conciliation. Little by little he succeeded in convincing his opponents of the need for radical changes in Scottish school education and more and more the Established Church was seen as being reactionary and obstinate. Yet it was driven by motives much less vindictive and much more altruistic than those of the Free Church or the United Presbyterians, both of which were willing to put religious instruction and the church's influence in schools at risk in the attempt to undermine the statutory position of the Established Church. As a result, in the 1861 Act all the Presbyterian Churches were losers and religious instruction was left exposed and vulnerable.

Appendix 4.1

ANY ASSESSMENT ON THE desire for education at this time should take into account the growing popularity of Evening Schools. Many of those who had left school early to go out to work later felt the need to further their education. Many of those who had left school early to go out to work later felt the need to further their education. Consider, for example, these statistics from the Census of 1851 showing the numbers and occupations of those attending Evening Schools.

Agricultural Laborers	561
Miners	249
Factory Operatives	2,397
Domestic Servants	553
Weavers	349
Bleachers	287
Warehousemen	278

In addition there were Printers, Shoemakers, Shopkeepers, Clerks, Fishermen, Seamen, Soldiers, Policemen, Architects, and Engineers. The majority of Evening Schools taught Reading, Writing, and Arithmetic, but many also taught history, book-keeping, navigation, physical science, and religious instruction. The Census recorded 11 which taught Modern Languages and 37 which taught Ancient Languages.

5

Legislating for a National System

THE SITUATION IN 1864

IN THE PERIOD 1864 to 1872 the most important developments for Scottish education were the Royal Commission set up in 1864 to inquire into schooling in Scotland and the Parliamentary legislation leading up to the Education (Scotland) Act of 1872. The Commission, under the chairmanship of the Duke of Argyll, began with fifteen members, with three more being added in December, 1865. Among its number were representatives from both houses of Parliament and members of both the Established Church and the Free Church of Scotland. There were Conservatives like Charles Baillie, MP for Linlithgowshire, who came from an old Scottish covenanting family, and Liberals like Alexander Murray Dunlop, MP for Greenock, a member of the Free Church and author of the "Claim of Right." The Dissenter, Adam Black, twice Lord Provost of Edinburgh, and Lord Belhaven, for many years Lord High Commissioner to the General Assembly of the Church of Scotland, were also members. For the next eight years much of the Education Committee's time would be devoted to assessing the importance for the Church of this Royal Commission's findings and responding to its recommendations and thereafter to the various Bills brought before Parliament by those who wished to see a national education system secured for Scotland once and for all.

As we have seen the 1861 Act failed to achieve the fully developed system of national education in Scotland that many had hoped for and Lord Advocate Moncreiff's further attempt in 1862 had failed through lack of support. The Established Church still retained a significant influence in the management of schools. The 1861 Act had conferred on presbyteries the right to present a complaint to the government if a schoolmaster contravened the prescribed declaration to uphold the teachings of the Westminster Confession and the doctrines of the Established Church. The Act also provided for the involvement of presbyteries where a schoolmaster was charged with immoral or cruel conduct or disqualified on the grounds of infirmity or inefficiency. Thus, in spite of the fact that the judicial function of presbyteries with regard to schools had been much curtailed, they retained considerable influence. Presbyteries continued visiting schools, parish and non-parish, and annually sent in comprehensive reports to the Education Committee. In 1865 the Church claimed that it had visited 1,004 parish schools and 1,593 others including Assembly schools, sessional schools, subscription schools and even schools run by dissenters. That old ways die hard has been well illustrated by A. J. Belford's description of the appointment of a teacher to a post in 1866:

> When George Andrews, who retired in 1913 from the headmastership of Gartconner School, Kirkintilloch, was appointed in 1866 he was examined by a committee of Waterside weavers in their aprons and shirt sleeves. He was asked to sing a psalm and told that hymns didn't count. Then he had to lead in prayer, and lastly had to give a discourse on the Prodigal Son. In terms of his appointment he had to whitewash the inside walls of the school once a year; pay feu-duty and all the rates as landlord; and give the school for preaching and funerals. He had to teach all the scholars, 120 of them, in one room, and on warm summer days had to take them outside where he worked in his shirt sleeves. He conducted an evening class, when the pupils brought their own pen and ink, their slates and pencils, and a candle, and a bottle to stick it in.[1]

While the Established Church continued to defend the system of parish and voluntary aided schools, in the country as a whole the support for a national non-denominational system continued to grow. Many saw it as the panacea for all political and social ills. The general dissatisfaction and the desire for change were regularly expressed in statements made to the Argyll Commission. James Taylor, a United Presbyterian minister from Glasgow and the education spokesman for that denomination, reminded the commission that opposition to the present system came not only

1. Belford, *Centenary Handbook of the Educational Institute of Scotland*, 113.

from his own denomination and that of the Free Church but also from Scottish MPs and from members of the Established Church itself. In the interviews conducted by the commission it was clear that for one reason or another few were happy with the existing scheme. Of those who gave oral or written evidence to the commission ninety-nine out of the 136 indicated that they favored a new system and of these forty-three were ministers and laymen of all denominations and thirty-five were teachers.

THE REPORTS AND FINDINGS OF THE ARGYLL COMMISSION

The Commission's remit was to offer an opinion on whether or not the funds voted by Parliament for school education in Scotland were being used beneficially and appropriately and to suggest how educational provision could be improved. One of the commission's first tasks was to ascertain as accurately as possible the existing state of education in Scotland. To obtain an independent over-all assessment of the educational provision the commission sent out schedules to registrars with the direction that when these had been completed they should be checked by the ministers connected with each school. Where a minister of any denomination disagreed with the registrar's figures he could return a separate schedule. The findings and recommendations of the commission were published in reports covering oral and written evidence given by 136 ministers and laymen of all denominations and written evidence submitted by Assistant Commissioners appointed to investigate the state of education in Elementary schools and in Burgh and Middle-class schools throughout the country. Glasgow was the only major city to be visited by the commissioners who considered it as offering a reasonable picture of the situation in a large urban area. From the information gathered in its cross-examination of witnesses and from an extensive examination of schools throughout the country, the commission reached a number of conclusions. On the basis of these it produced its recommendations and draft education Bill. A number of these recommendations had a direct bearing on the Established Church's involvement with schools.

Report on Schools and Teaching

In 1866 Assistant Commissioners Thomas Harvey, who three years later was elected as rector of Edinburgh Academy, and Alexander Craig Sellar, who was to become a Liberal MP, were appointed to carry out a survey of burgh and middle-class schools. They submitted their report at the end of 1867. At the same time HMI Daniel Fearon, who had been taking part in the Schools Inquiry Commission in England, was sent to Scotland to investigate the state of middle class education in Scotland and make a comparison with the same class of schools in England. The Commission defined middle-class schools as schools where pupils left when they were sixteen years of age.

These commissioners found that over-all, the burgh and other secondary schools of Scotland were in a satisfactory condition, and superior to the majority of the English Grammar schools.[2] They reported that the number of pupils attending Secondary schools in Scotland was significantly higher than in France or England. It was reported that 71 percent of teachers in middle-class schools had been to university though not all had graduated and only 10 percent had attended a Normal school. The report maintained that the connection between the Parish and Burgh schools and the Universities was an essential element in Scottish education and argued that any changes which might be made in the education system should be aimed at strengthening the connection between the Universities and the schools.

From the statistics submitted by the registrars and ministers the commission concluded that, with 1 in 6·5 of the whole population on school rolls, whatever might be the case in individual districts, the lack of schools was not as great as had been generally supposed and that whatever might be the quality of the education given, Scotland was well supplied with teachers. Naturally the Education Committee welcomed this finding as supporting the existing system. The commission concluded, nevertheless, that averages such as 1 in 6·5 of the population concealed the true state of affairs in particular localities where the percentage of children attending school was much lower. In the view of the Kirk's Education Committee, however, the reliability of the commission's calculations of the percentage of children attending school suffered from the fact that there was no consistency with regard to the age when children were taken as starting school. They could point, for example, to reports submitted by Sellar and C. F. Maxwell, appointed to examine schools in the Lowlands, who counted the number of children between the ages of three or four

2. This is one of the first usages of the term "secondary" applied to schools in Scotland. These were schools teaching beyond the elementary stage, normally in burgh and middle-class schools but also in parish and Assembly schools.

and fifteen while acknowledging that in Scotland it was not the custom to send children to school much before they were five or six years of age and that they might leave at any age between six and sixteen. The commission concluded that while many of the denominational schools made a valuable contribution to school education on the whole the efficiency of non-parish schools was very unequal and the whole system was unreliable. Based only on its inquiry into the state of education in Glasgow, it judged that the facts obtained proved that the voluntary system was totally inadequate in its provision for the population in the large towns.

It was evident from the reports that lack of schools was not the main problem. (The main exception to this was the Western Highlands and Islands. Sheriff Nicolson, being himself a Highlander and a Gaelic speaker, was appointed as Assistant Commissioner to report on the state of education in the Hebrides. His report underlined the difficulties of establishing schools in scattered communities where people were predominantly Gaelic-speaking. He reached the conclusion that some 230 more schools were needed there.) Although the need of more schools might have been the case in some rural and urban areas, much of the evidence only confirmed what was already well known, that under the existing system poor attendance meant that schools were not being fully utilized. Many of the poorest children attended school only irregularly and few stayed on at school beyond the age of twelve. The commission were informed that in Glasgow only one in three children of school age actually attended school. This was blamed on the inability of the denominational system to erect enough schools, on the fees being too high, and on parents having to send their children out to work. While the commission would have liked to see some form of compulsory education introduced, it admitted that this was impractical at that time. It contented itself with pointing out that many of the representatives interviewed had been in favor of extending the Factory Acts to cover rural districts and new industries such as the tobacco works in Glasgow, and expressed its opinion that such an extension would be desirable.

The condition of school buildings and the standard of teaching were also subject to scrutiny by the Assistant Commissioners and gave cause for concern. Here the situation in the Hebrides proved to be the most worrying with 52 percent of the buildings needing to be repaired or rebuilt. In Glasgow school premises and the standard of teaching were reported as "good" in 72 percent of the schools examined. In the rest of the country 71 percent of the buildings in the schools visited were considered "good" or "fair" and over 71 percent of the teaching was found to be more than adequate.

With regard to elementary education the commissioners concluded that it was on the whole better than was generally anticipated, but it still left considerable room for improvement. The main defects, they stated, were poor organization and the lack of supervision by some competent central authority. Figures were produced showing that in 1864 in Scottish schools standards in writing and arithmetic (though not in reading) were inferior to those in England. They did concede, however, that, unlike the situation in England, the mass of the Scottish population in the rural districts had received some basic education and this was taken into account in this calculation. Indeed, the superiority of the parish system in Scotland was demonstrated by an examination of the percentage of men and women able to sign the marriage registers in 1855 and in 1861. Comparing Scotland with England, it was calculated that in 1855 88·6 percent of the men, and 77·2 percent of the women, in Scotland had signed the marriage register in writing; while in England, in the same year, the percentage was only 70·5 percent of men and 58·8 percent of women. In 1861 the percentage in England was somewhat larger, but Scotland still showed a decided superiority. In some rural towns and counties the percentages were even higher thus in Peebles 100 percent of the men who married in 1861 signed the register in writing, and in Dumfries it was 97 percent.

With regard to the proficiency of teachers the commission agreed that while Normal school training was useful, by itself it was inadequate for anyone teaching above elementary level where a university education was what mattered most. Indeed it was rather scathing in its estimation of Normal schools:

> The Normal-school stamp of a man is inferior as an intellectual type to the well-trained university man. Their method of teaching is too contracted for the higher class of schools. In Elementary schools, the originality and power of mind which are fostered and brought out by a successful course of university instruction are not essential, or at least the absence of these qualities is not remarked. But in schools professing a secondary education, where the scholars are older and more advanced, the narrowing influence of exclusively Normal-school training, and the stereotyped method of instruction derived from it, are at once apparent and do

not appear to be productive of good results. For the younger and more elementary classes in the Burgh and Middle-class schools, Normal-school men might profitably be employed as assistants.[3]

So much for the importance of teachers being trained in "the art of teaching"! The Commission apparently did not think much of the considerable investment made in Normal schools both by the Church and the government nor does it seem to have appreciated the broad curriculum undertaken by many teachers in training.

In spite of what would appear to be reasonably satisfactory results the commission concluded that, taking into account the number of children not at school, the quality of teaching and the state of the buildings on the whole the parish system had proved to be inadequate, especially in the towns, and required upgrading. Much of the blame, it was held, lay with the churches and the supervision of presbyteries, a conclusion which touched at the very heart of matters fundamental to the role of the Established Church.

The Denominational System and the Supervision of Presbyteries.

Could religious instruction be secured without the supervision of presbyteries and the denominational system and did the parish minister need to be *ex officio* on any local management committee? Addressing these questions took up much of the Commission's time and the opinions given were many and varied. Naturally there were representatives of the Established Church who held strongly to the view that presbyteries still had a necessary and useful role to play in maintaining standards and encouraging a positive ethos. Men like John Cook, convener of the Assembly's Education Committee, and William Muir, a former convener who had resigned in 1849 in protest at the committee's acceptance of government grants, held that presbytery examinations were efficient and that the influence of the Church was necessary to ensure the survival of religious education. Not all associated with the Established Church shared this view. William Stevenson, Professor of Ecclesiastical History in Edinburgh University and formerly a parish minister in Arbroath and in South Leith,

---

3. Argyll Commission, *Third Report, Report of the Assistant-Commissioners on the State of Education in the Burgh and Middle-Class schools in Scotland*, 79. Two years after it was set up the Commission appointed "Assistant Commissioners" who did the actual legwork of going round the schools and collecting information. Their findings are the substance of the *Third Report*.

told the commission that he was of the opinion that the denominational system had no practical advantage and only encouraged jealous rivalry. Even Simon Laurie, the secretary of the General Assembly's Education Committee, was a little ambivalent about presbytery supervision which he regarded as useful in stimulating the efforts of the teachers and children but which was really of little value in testing the quality of the learning and teaching. On all sides there was agreement that the denominational system was not an important factor for most parents. Thomas Guthrie, whose great passion was for Ragged Schools and a Bible education for the poor, claimed that the people of Scotland would send their children to the school where they believed education in the three Rs was the best and that they would not send children to a school where the Bible was not taught. James Taylor, from the United Presbyterian Church, supported this view and maintained that in Scotland people persisted in sending their children to the best school no matter to what denomination it belonged. In its findings the commission reached same conclusion and noted that, apart from in Roman Catholic schools, religious instruction was much the same whatever denomination ran the school, so there was no reason on religious grounds why there should not be a national system.

With regard to the importance of presbytery visits to schools the commission found that while the annual examination tended to increase the general interest which both parents and children took in education nevertheless throughout the country teachers were of the view that presbytery examinations were of little practical value and that this was an opinion shared by parents, heritors, and even a few of the clergy. So much depended on the character of the local minister and the active interest he took in the management of the school. The commission claimed that this conclusion was confirmed by their own independent examinations of a number of Assembly schools, the results of which indicated that these schools did not perform nearly as well as the reports from presbyteries had led them to expect. It was admitted, however, that compared to other denominations the standard of instruction in the Parish and Church of Scotland (Assembly) schools was, if anything, superior.

THE ARGYLL COMMISSION'S RECOMMENDATIONS
AND DRAFT BILL

Proposals for Improvement

To upgrade the provision of school education the commission proposed
to set up a Central Board with powers to establish as many new schools as
might be required throughout the country. Much as it might have wanted,
the commission realized that it would be impractical to accept immediate
financial responsibility for all the schools supported by voluntary effort
yet it could not leave them untouched. At the same time it was necessary to establish new schools and there was pressure from those who had
given evidence to change the way parish schools were managed and to
abolish denominational schools. The commission's solution was to set up
a system which, at least for a time, would incorporate old and new with
the hope that eventually all schools would be brought under the Central
Board. New schools would be financed partly by local assessment and
partly by government grants and would be open to children of every
class and denomination. The Board would impose on ratepayers the sum
it needed for the new schools and would decide which schools would
qualify for government grants. It would employ special commissioners
to visit schools in addition to regular inspectors and would have the
power to inquire into the efficiency of teachers and to dismiss a teacher
without appeal. Schoolmasters would no longer hold their posts *ad vitam aut culpam*. The schools established by the Board would be called
"New National" schools, and would be part of a national system. In the
rural parishes they would be managed by school committees one half of
the membership being drawn from the landed proprietors and heritors
and the other half elected by the ratepayers. In the burghs school committees were to be nominated by the town councils. Under this system
teachers would have been answerable to three bodies, a Central Board,
the Local School Committee and to the Privy Council through its Scotch
Department which would control the inspection of schools. As part of
its strategy the commission decided that, for the time being at least, it
would not tamper with the existing management of parish schools where
the qualification for heritors to sit on the board would remain the same
and the parish minister would continue as an *ex officio* member. The
Commission proposed that all schoolmasters would be required to hold
a government certificate of competency and would be selected without

regard to their Church affiliation. A minimum salary of thirty-five pounds exclusive of fees was proposed. It was intended that parish schools would for a time be designated as "Old National" schools but with the agreement of the majority of the local management committee (the heritors and the minister) they could be brought under the authority of the Central Board as "Adopted National" schools while retaining their existing system of management. Other schools, including denominational schools, could—again with the consent of the management committee—become part of the new system as "Adopted National" schools. They would still be funded from voluntary sources and if found to be efficient by inspectors could still claim parliamentary grants. Further Old National and Adopted National schools could become New National schools if two-thirds of the existing management committee agreed. Where New National schools were set up or others adopted, the local committee would appoint teachers and fix the curriculum and hours of instruction. The Committee of Council would continue to inspect all parish schools and all schools in receipt of grants and offering elementary education, but inspectors could be of any religious denomination. The commission recommended that no new denominational schools set up two years after the passing of the Act should receive government funding.

As for religious instruction the commission, having heard a considerable body of evidence in favor of continuing this in schools, left the matter very much as it was but introduced a Conscience Clause which gave parents the statutory right to withdraw their children from any religious teaching to which they objected. Where existing parish or denominational schools were adopted as New National schools or where New National schools were established, the local school committee would decide whether or not to include religious instruction on the curriculum. Where they decided to have religious instruction, however, it would not be subject to government inspection. The commission proposed that the Revised Code which had been introduced into Scotland in May 1864[4] with the examination of children in the three Rs should be fully implemented apart from a section which had limited government funding to children from the working-class. The commission agreed that this did not do justice to the situation in Scotland where historically all social classes had made use of the educational provision.

4. In Scotland the Revised Code was suspended after six weeks with the appointment of the Argyll Commission.

The Argyll Commission's Draft Bill

In May 1867 a Bill was drafted incorporating these recommendations—
"A Bill to Extend and Improve the Parochial schools of Scotland, and to
make further Provision for the Education of the People of Scotland." The
Bill indicated a reluctance to introduce a fully implemented national system too quickly. As a compromise it contained the seeds of conflict. The
denominational system remained but the new Board could declare a denominational school unnecessary and a Church would then need to object
on behalf of its school. Presumably by introducing the Conscience Clause
and by taking religious instruction out of the compulsory curriculum the
commissioners hoped to please the dissenters and the secularists. By implementing the Revised Code and making it necessary for all teachers to
hold a government certificate of efficiency they believed they could raise
the standard of elementary education and so increase school attendance.
By creating a Scotch department it went some way towards distancing
Scottish education from what was seen by many as the Anglicizing influence of the Privy Council but it is doubtful if it went far enough to satisfy
those who were concerned about the erosion of Scottish culture and the
Scottish education tradition. The commission appeared anxious to win
over the Churches and in particular the Established Church. It recognized
the contribution of the voluntary-supported schools and allowed parish
ministers to remain on parish school committees. Parish schools and denominational schools, where found efficient and necessary by inspectors,
would still be able to claim parliamentary grants. These concessions, however, did little to convince the Assembly's Education Committee that the
proposals would be to the benefit of Scottish education and the Church
was not slow to identify what it regarded as the weaknesses and inconsistencies of the commission's proposals. In its objections the Established
Church had the support of the increasingly strong Educational Institute
of Scotland and of the Committee of Parochial Schoolmasters both of
which agreed that Scottish schools should be administered by a Scottish
Board without any reference to the Privy Council.

Church Responses to the Recommendations
and Bill of the Argyll Commission

The Education Committee responded to the Argyll Commission in two
major reports, a "Special Report Showing the Nature and Effect of the

Recommendations and Draft Bill" which was made available to the 1867 General Assembly and "Remarks on the Recommendations and Draft Bill" drawn up by the Convener, John Cook, which was published in the December of that year and incorporated in the committee's report to the Assembly in 1868. The former offered the committee's initial reaction to the First and Second Reports of the Commission which had covered Country Districts and Elementary Schools. The *Remarks* followed the completion of the commission's Report on Burgh and Middle-class Schools in December 1867. With regard to the findings of the commission the Education Committee claimed that the reports added little to what was already common knowledge namely that the parish and denominational schools were not sectarian and had encouraged tolerance and as a rule were efficient, and that schools not in receipt of government grants such as Adventure schools, were in poor condition and badly taught. That the commission had identified deficiencies in the Scottish education system should not have surprised anyone, Cook commented, since no one involved in establishing schools ever imagined that one school in every parish would be enough to meet the educational needs of the country. Indeed, that was why denominational and subscription schools had been set up and not, as some had claimed, out of denominational rivalry.

The committee reported to the 1867 Assembly that the Bill's proposals were even more objectionable than those of Moncreiff's 1862 Bill because they involved the eventual dismantling of the whole parish system and abolishing of denominational and voluntary supported schools. Further, in its opinion, the conclusions were based on mistaken calculations and in some cases seemed to fly in the face of the findings contained in the Commission's own reports. The committee pointed to what it saw as some glaring inconsistencies in the commission's proposals. There was the matter of the different age-groups the commissioners had considered in calculating the number of children attending school and the different conclusions it had reached as a result. Again, on the one hand the commission had admitted that the simplest way to increase the provision of education would be to extend and improve the existing parish school system and recommended that there should be no change to the existing management of parish schools or church schools, it being too expensive for the state to take these over. On the other hand, the Education Committee pointed out, the commissioners had gone on to suggest that a parish school, if agreed at a meeting of the heritors and minister, might be converted into a New National school where the management would be in the hands of a school committee. According to the Church, these proposals for adopting schools into the new national system had only been made in order to meet those few cases where ministers or heritors had little interest in a school, or to relieve heritors of their financial responsibilities. In spite of its assertions that the most desirable and the simplest solution would be the extension of the parish system the commission was proposing to do the opposite. In their examination of subscription schools the commissioners had laid the inefficiency of these at the door of the management of the school being in the hands of the parents of the children, or boards elected by them. However, commented the Assembly's committee, surely the constitution of the new local committees would be no different. Any proposals to further involve ratepayers in school management ran counter to the commission's own findings that in many places ratepayers were apathetic as far as parish matters were concerned.

The Education Committee believed that religious instruction would be put at risk by leaving it to the new school committees to decide if it should be available, by removing the need for teachers to enter into any kind of religious agreement, and by making the subject no longer open to inspection. This was at odds with one of the main conditions on which Committee of Council grants had been made to schools since its inception in 1839, namely that grants would only be made where religious instruction was included in the curriculum. It was pointed out that this principle had been restated in 1861 in the regulations issued with the Revised Code—regulations which were actually noted in the Commission's own report. The committee maintained that by removing the *ad vitam aut culpam* condition of appointment the schoolmaster would no longer have any security of tenure nor would he or she enjoy the social prestige which went with this kind of appointment.

In correspondence with Patrick Cumin, the secretary to the Royal Commission, the convener of the Education Committee took the Assistant Commissioners to task for assuming that an examination of the schools in Glasgow would provide sufficient data to cover all the manufacturing towns throughout the country. The committee claimed that the figures published showing the lack of school accommodation in Glasgow were not only inaccurate but gave a wrong impression of the educational needs in the large towns of Scotland. Glasgow was not typical and it was wrong to assume that the proportion of children on the school-roll in the large burghs of Scotland would generally be the same as that in Glasgow.

Throughout the Church there were fears that any application of the Revised Code with its emphasis on examination in the three *R*s would lower standards in Scottish schools. Teachers would concentrate on the subjects they were being paid for teaching. The more advanced subjects would be neglected threatening the Scottish tradition whereby able pupils were prepared to go to university straight from school. One schoolmaster published a short but scathing critique of the Argyll Commission's Report and the Bill which had accompanied it, echoing the sentiments of many in the Church. For him the Revised Code demanded only "a miserable modicum of reading, writing, and arithmetic . . . in reality no education at all . . . that education which influences and moulds the mind only begins where the Code ends."[5]

The reaction of the Established Church to the Argyll Commission was summed up in the closing words of the 1867 Special Report which called on the General Assembly to oppose a Bill that offered no security for religious instruction, discouraged all voluntary effort, and offered no help to teachers. On a more constructive note the Education Committee offered a number of positive suggestions for dealing with the present educational deficiency. These took into account some of the Commission's ideas and included the setting up of a Scottish Board of Education under the Privy Council which would be based in Edinburgh and would administer a Scotch Parliamentary Grant. This Board would put pressure on heritors to provide new schools. Where heritors refused to co-operate, the Board would have powers to raise the necessary funding by assessing all occupants and proprietors in the parish, who would then share in the management of the schools. In rural areas where local rating could not meet the costs, the denominational system could be extended with the Churches receiving further government grants. This way forward would increase the number of schools while preserving the parish system and the Church's role in it.

---

5. *A Plea for the Parish Schools by a Parochial Schoolmaster*, 8 and 23.

FURTHER ATTEMPTS AT REFORM

Parochial Schools (Scotland) Bill (1869)

The Commission's Bill was never progressed further. It suffered a fate common to much Scottish Parliamentary business, namely having to give way to the pressure of other business which in this decade included Parliamentary Reform. Early in February 1869, however, the Duke of Argyll, described as "a Liberal who was an Established Churchman . . . well placed to engineer a compromise," took up the matter again counting, no doubt, on the large number of Scottish Liberal MPs who had been returned to parliament at the first election after the 1868 Reform Act and who were likely to favor a non-denominational system of national education. His Parochial Schools Bill was introduced into the House of Lords in February 1869 but it did not reach the Commons until July. Two factors impeded the progress of this Bill. There was the consideration that any changes to the Scottish situation might affect changes to the proposals to reform the English school system which were being discussed at this time, and the government was anxious to see its Irish Disestablishment Act safely on the statute book. With regard to the former the government found itself in the difficult position of having to satisfy the demand of two very active teachers' organizations which took up opposing positions, The National Education Union and the National Education League. The National Education Union was the more conservative and nearer to the Established Church of Scotland's own position. It denied that the educational deficiency in England was as great as some were suggesting and believed in keeping denominational schools, while the National Education League was in favor of change. The English historian Llewellyn Woodward believed that the Reform Act had made the education of the masses an urgent problem with the supporters of "unsectarian" education, mainly from the National Education League, trying to force the government to give up the denominational principle.[6]

In his opening speech to the Lords in February, 1869, Argyll explained that he proposed to deal with the great defects in Scottish education—deficiencies in cities and in rural areas, defective school buildings and the removal of bad teachers. In fact the Bill was in many respects

---

6. Woodward, *The Age of Reform 1815–1870*, 482. The Newcastle Commission (1858) had examined elementary education, and the Taunton Commission (1864) had reported on the need for secondary schools.

almost identical to the Argyll Commission's Draft Bill but with a number of important amendments. There was still to be a Scottish Board of Education but now there was an attempt to ensure that Board members would have a better grasp of the educational scene and be less dominated by the government. This Board would have included a representative of the EIS so that for the first time the voice of the teaching profession would be heard at this level. One later amendment revived the conviction that in appointing teachers not only should their academic qualifications be taken into account but also their skill in the theory and practice of teaching which, of course, the Commission's own report had belittled. Argyll believed that the power to dismiss teachers should belong to the national Board and not to the local school committees. He also wanted to amend the Revised Code by extending its provisions to include payment by results in the higher branches of education. One change which was to prove unacceptable to the Lords, many of whom were from the landed gentry, was his proposal that where new schools were set up in the rural parishes, only one third of the membership of the local school committees should be elected by heritors and landowners and that the other two-thirds should be elected by the ratepayers.

Argyll's Bill divided the Church and the country. A Commission of the General Assembly meeting in March 1869 decided that it was not much different from the Argyll Commission's Bill of 1867 and agreed to oppose it on the same grounds. There were a number of commissioners, however, who would have been happy to support the Bill had some security for religious instruction been offered and at the Assembly in May a minority wanted the Church to give its backing to a national rather than a denominational system of education and approve the Bill. This support for the move towards a national scheme was also to be found throughout Church where there was a surprising amount of agreement with what the Duke of Argyll's Bill was attempting to achieve. Two of the largest synods in the country took up opposing stances. The Synod of Perth and Stirling approved of the object of the Bill and of its provisions to extend education subject to religious instruction and the religious character of the teachers being guaranteed while the Synod of Glasgow and Ayr came out strongly against the Bill claiming that it subverted the present management of parish schools. A meeting of ministers, elders and members of the Church of Scotland held in Glasgow in March 1869 agreed with general object of the Bill and approved of the setting up of a Board of Education for

Scotland and of new national schools but it parted company with Argyll when it came to converting parish and denominational schools into national schools and considered that to discourage voluntary efforts and relieve heritors of the need to make the statutory provisions would throw an unnecessary financial burden on ratepayers.

In organizations not directly connected with the Church there was some support for the Education Committee's stance. The General Council of the University of Glasgow resolved that the existing system of school education should continue and that the "use and wont" of religious teaching in Scotland should not be endangered. The Coal and Iron Masters in the West of Scotland petitioned the Lords against the Bill. They wanted the schools erected and maintained by them to remain as they were. They claimed these works' schools had been successful, that they had been founded for the purpose of giving religious education and that this had always been harmoniously carried out and that much would be lost by converting them into new national schools. It would appear that the Educational Institute in opposing the Bill shared many of the Church's concerns. From 1868 to 1869 *The Museum* published several articles by members of the EIS all critical of the Bill's treatment of schoolmasters and supporting the retention of religious instruction in the curriculum. Typical was the attitude of a speaker addressing the Cupar Branch who claimed, "A new lord is to be created for us—a general board—armed with unlimited scope for its amusement in suspending and withdrawing teachers' certificates . . . We cannot, therefore, view with anything but alarm the efforts that are being made by some parties to alter the constitution of the schools, and to impair their efficiency, if not to endanger their existence, by separating religion from secular instruction."[7]

It was now clear that opinion in the Church was gradually changing. By the summer of 1869 the Education Committee had moved to a position where it accepted schools being financed through local assessment where there was no other way of providing the necessary funding, and management by local school committees elected by properly qualified ratepayers. It even accepted the imposition of the conscience clause recognizing that in practice this had always been allowed for in Church of Scotland schools. Indeed, the committee could claim that the Bill as a whole had their approval in all save two respects—the proposals for "converting"

7. "The Recommendations and Draft Bill—A Speech delivered by Mr Borrowman, of Auchtermuchty, at the Cupar Branch of the Educational Institute," 415–16.

parish schools into "New National" schools, and the absence of provision for Religious Instruction. For the first time we find the proposal that religious instruction should be legislated for according to "use and wont," a phrase which would unfortunately be omitted from the preamble to the 1872 Education Bill: "The Committee respectfully urge on the attention of members of Parliament the importance of inserting as a preamble to the conscience clause the words '*in every New National School religious instruction shall be given in conformity with the use and wont of the Parish Schools of Scotland*.'" The committee believed that it was now time to unite with the Free Church in urging the government to acknowledge the importance of religious instruction in schools. It recognized that it was unlikely to succeed in achieving its objectives through amendments to Argyll's Bill and consoled itself with the thought that, whereas in England there were fears that changes in the Scottish system might lead to unwanted changes to the English education system, Scotland might actually benefit from what was being proposed in England.

In the end Argyll's plan to reform the school education system in Scotland was thwarted, not by the Church of Scotland, but by his fellow peers who belonged to other denominations. The Earl of Denbigh, speaking on behalf of the Roman Catholics in Scotland, argued that the Bill had been drawn up by Presbyterians for the benefit of Presbyterians and that both the Episcopalian and Catholics who wanted to retain management of their denominational schools, would alike suffer if it was approved. He eventually attempted to introduce a new clause to the effect that nothing in the Bill should apply to the education of Roman Catholic or Episcopalian children in Scotland. As a result the Lords amended the Bill to permit all denominational schools to claim parliamentary grants without having to become Adopted schools. The Duke of Marlborough objected to the reduced influence of heritors in electing the school committees. The Duke of Richmond (always in sympathy with the Established Church of Scotland and in 1885 to become the first Secretary for Scotland) claimed that the way school committees were to be appointed would lead to endless squabbles and dissensions about religious education. He believed that the state of education in Scotland was by no means unsatisfactory and that the Bill struck directly at the old parochial system which, in combination with the voluntary system, had worked to the benefit of all. The Archbishop of Canterbury, defending the denominational system, maintained that England would not accept a conscience clause since that might turn denominational schools into national schools. Disraeli made a late intervention in the debate and argued that "anything connected with Scotch education is not merely a Scotch question, but one of national interest, and one on which the House ought to be fully acquainted, with the proposals of the Government, and the motives which influence them." To this the Lord Advocate replied caustically that he welcomed the interest of such a distinguished member but "should have been glad if that interest had been developed a little earlier in the Session."[8]

Eventually Argyll's Bill had to be abandoned by the Lords due to lack of time and political disputes, a rather unsatisfactory conclusion to an important debate. All things considered, with some readjustment this Bill might well have found acceptance in the Commons and in Scotland. The Bill's rejection by the Lords, however, was more than just an expression of party political animosity. Moves to change the English system were now well advanced and those who opposed change were concerned about the effect any success in introducing changes to Scotland might have on English opinion. As it happened a year later Parliament passed a Bill introduced by W. E. Forster the person in charge of the education department in England. Forster took English elementary schools in the direction which Argyll had wanted for Scotland with locally elected school boards being given the power to levy rates, build schools, provide teachers, and even, where appropriate, make school attendance compulsory. Where schools were managed by elected school boards any religious instruction was to be non-denominational. On the other hand denominational schools were left as they were in areas where they were working well and met local needs, and grants to these schools were increased.

It might have been expected that with the failure of Argyll's Bill and the passing of the English Education Act of 1870, another attempt to reform Scottish education would soon have followed. In fact it was not until February 1871 that fresh efforts were made to introduce a national system to Scotland. Among the reasons for this eighteen-month delay was the change in the Lord Advocate's post, George Young taking over from James Moncreiff in October 1869. Another, and probably more important reason, was the time and attention that had been taken up with the debate on the English Elementary Education. It is likely that Young was holding back to assess what impact the changes to the English system

8. Hansard, 3rd Series, vol. 196.

would have in Scotland. In finally rejecting Argyll's Bill the Church lost its last chance to retain its hold on Scottish education and to preserve the distinctive identity of Scottish schools. The point has been succinctly put by J. D. Myers: "The bill of 1869 [Parochial Schools] can be seen as the last distinctively Scottish educational reform measure of the period. It was, in its conception and general outline, more similar to the bill of 1854, for example, than either was to the bills of 1871 and 1872 which were significantly less Scottish in spirit and approach. Lord Advocate George Young, had a considerably different attitude to the task from James Moncreiff and was less sympathetically attuned to the distinctive national characteristic of the Scottish tradition."[9]

The Continuing Debate in Scotland

Although no new legislation affecting Scottish schools was introduced until 1871 national education was still a live issue and agitation for change found expression in many quarters with the place of religious instruction remaining the most disputed topic. Even before the close of 1869, Edinburgh City Council was calling on the Government to bring forward legislation to provide a non-sectarian and non-denominational system with a General Board of Education in Scotland elected by public bodies. There was to be an end to denominational grants and a clause making education compulsory. The magistrates of Leith suggested that MPs for the counties and burghs of Scotland should represent the electorate on any Board of Education, while Musselburgh Town Council agreed that while the Bible should be retained in the schools the reading of it should be decided by the Local School Committee, and a conscience clause should be operated.[10] A public meeting held in Glasgow to discuss the place of the Bible in schools resolved that in primary education Bible instruction should be given while respecting the conscientious objections of parents and guardians. In Edinburgh those seeking to improve conditions for the poor agreed that any Education Bill should extend the terms of the Factory Acts, making education compulsory for all children under fourteen and should legislate for the provision of industrial training schools.

Teachers continued to voice anxieties about the application of the Revised Code and in particular its effect on the teaching of more

9. Myers, "Scottish Nationalism and the Antecedents of the 1872 Education Act," 86.
10. NAS AD56, 47/3 and 47/4.

advanced subjects. One writer expressed concern that science subjects were neglected. The same writer argued that religion should be taught in Sunday Schools and that cramming pupils' heads with the Shorter Catechism and using the Bible as a text-book had little to do with moral education. Indeed, he claimed, "whisky and Catechism are the two greatest curses of Scotland."

Another issue which was beginning to emerge at this time in discussions about education was the possible reunion of the denominations. In the words of the Scottish advocate and historian G. W. T. Omond (1846–1929), "the ashes of the disruption fires were turning cold."[11] In 1867 the Moderator of the General Assembly of the Established Church had called for the reunion of all Scottish Presbyterians and by 1870 there was widespread support for the abolition of patronage. That year the Presbytery of Dunkeld overtured the General Assembly to consider adopting measures which might accomplish a union between the Church of Scotland and those Evangelical Churches which substantially agreed with it both in doctrine and government. Similarly the Presbytery of Forfar asked the Assembly to enter into discussions with the other Presbyterian Churches in Scotland noting that the existing divisions fostered a spirit of sectarianism and put obstacles in the way of ensuring that study of the Scriptures was part of any national system of education. The significance of these calls for Church union for any future Education Bill was that both the Kirk and the Free Church would be able to speak with one voice in favor of religious instruction in Scottish schools.[12]

Young's Education (Scotland) Bill (1871)

In February 1871 Lord Advocate Young presented in the Commons his Education (Scotland) Bill—"A Bill to extend and amend the provisions of the law of Scotland on the subject of education." It was clear from the title of this Bill that it was going to be a radical departure from the attempts at reform made by Lord Moncreiff and the Duke of Argyll. All previous Bills had been classified as "Parochial Schools" Bills with the intent of improving the traditional parish school system, but the wording of this Bill made

11. Omond, *The Lord Advocates of Scotland*, 295.

12. Free Church minister James Begg, who had violently opposed the union of his Church with the United Presbyterians, and Norman MacLeod, who was a keen supporter of Church reunion, found common ground at the Glasgow meeting on the place of the Bible in the School referred to above.

it clear that Young's aim was to introduce legislation for a completely new educational set-up. Young's stated intention was to provide an efficient system of education which would be available to the everyone.

The Bill provided for a committee of the Privy Council to be called the Scottish Education Department. Schools were to be called "parish schools" and "burgh schools" and infant and evening schools were to be established. Attendance at school was to be compulsory for all children between five and thirteen years of age. School boards would be elected in each parish and burgh by all owners or occupiers of lands or heritages of the annual value of not less than four pounds. These boards would be responsible for managing schools and appointing teachers, but the power to dismiss teachers lay with the Scottish Education Department whose decision would be final and not reviewable. Schools erected or maintained by voluntary contributions and by the Churches could transfer into the new system but this was not made compulsory. No recommendation was made about the place of religious instruction in the curriculum but there would be no grant for religious instruction and a conscience clause allowed for the withdrawal of children from instruction in religious subjects and on any day set apart for religious observance.[13]

From within the Established Church there was the usual flurry of resolutions opposing the Bill. Edinburgh Presbytery claimed that where ratepayers had to fund schooling they would only be interested in spending as little as they could and this in turn was bound to lower the standard of education. The Education Committee continued to plead for the continuation of the old parish system and for a secure place for religious instruction on the curriculum. It again claimed that the deficiencies in Scotland were not as great as was asserted (and certainly not as great as those in England which the Education Act there had attempted to put right) and that new education boards should only be set up where serious needs had been identified. Outside the Churches there was a mixed reaction to this new Bill. As far as the management of schools was concerned there was opposition to Scottish education being controlled from London and to the continuation of grants to denominational schools but there was a general acceptance of local school boards. It was clear that in Scotland many people considered that if congregations were now thought competent to elect their minister, ratepayers should be just as able to elect

---

13. Here "religious observance" is introduced for the first time. Its inclusion here would be of significance for later legislation, particularly in the twentieth century.

the schoolmaster. In June 1871, Young, having received notice of two hundred amendments to his Bill, decided to withdraw it but by February 1872 he was back with another very similar one.

THE EDUCATION (SCOTLAND) ACT (1872)

In drafting his new Bill Young made some important changes and some notable amendments were made before the Bill became law in August 1872. A Board of Education for Scotland was to be set up for three years with a possible extension of another two years and would meet in Edinburgh. It would consist of five members appointed by the government. With a few exceptions burgh as well as parish schools became "public schools." The historic role of the heritors was abolished with the management of schools and the appointment of teachers becoming the responsibility of locally elected school boards in every parish and burgh. All jurisdiction, powers and authority, such as the right to visit and inspect schools, by presbyteries or other church courts were abolished. The Act introduced compulsory school attendance for all children from five to thirteen years of age and insisted that teachers should hold a certificate of competency awarded by a Scotch Education Department. Funding, for all except denominational schools, was to come from government grants, local rates and school fees. The Bill emphasized that school boards should promote the teaching of secondary level subjects, however, the very schools which offered pupils the higher branches of knowledge and not just the three Rs such as the ancient burgh schools and academies were not covered by the Act. These higher class public schools were left to be funded by town councils and from fees and were not to be examined by government inspectors. Schools such as these might have helped to extend secondary education in Scotland and it was one of the great defects of the 1872 Act that they were not included in the new system. Existing denominational schools which were deemed to be efficiently meeting the needs of the parish or burgh would continue to receive government grants except for building purposes. New ones were to receive grants only where they could be shown to be essential to meet a particular need which could not be met by the parish schools. In future parliamentary grants would be given only to schools which the Scotch Education Department deemed necessary to meet the religious beliefs of parents. For Roman Catholic and Episcopalian schools this meant instruction in doctrines particular to these Churches. Denominational schools such as Assembly and Society schools, taught by uncertificated masters would not be inspected and would not receive any government funding. As far as religious instruction was concerned, where a school board decided it should be provided, it was to be given either at the beginning or at the end of the day to make it easier for parents to withdraw children as allowed by the conscience clause, but there would no funding for it. By way of clarification the Lord Advocate said that "the object of the clause was that there should be a religious observance both at the commencement and at the end of the secular instruction."

In February 1872 the Church's Education Committee issued a statement on the provisions of this new Bill which more or less adopted the same arguments as those used to oppose the 1871 Bill. This time round, however, Lord Young had a powerful Scottish ally in the influential Free Churchman Dr Thomas Guthrie:

> I have all along advocated a National as opposed to a Denominational system; thinking that we have divisions more than enough in the Church without exasperating their bitterness by introducing them into the School. . . . I have always recommended a system much like that the Lord Advocate's Bill embodies. Can any man in his senses believe that the Bible-reading, Bible-loving people of Scotland will thrust the Word of God out of their schools? Lend your hearty support to a Bill which, conserving all that is good in our Parochial schools, will carry the blessings of education into every mining district, dark lane of the city, and lone highland glen.[14]

Guthrie's view was not held generally in the Free Church which like the Established Church held out for the statutory provision of religious instruction and there were some MPs who supported the stance taken up by these Churches and who did not think that the decision about the provision of religious instruction should be left to local school committees. The Established Church's Education Committee did make one concession in the hope of achieving a compromise with regard to the management of parish schools. It suggested that the constitution of the boards managing these schools, presently the heritors paying a rental of more than £100 and the parish minister, might be widened to include representatives of all who contributed towards the upkeep of a school.

14. Guthrie, *The Scotch Education Bill*, 1, 2 & 4.

It is to the Scottish judge Edward S. Gordon, Dean of the Faculty of Advocates and Conservative MP for the Universities of Glasgow and Aberdeen, that we are indebted for moving an addition to the Preamble which would eventually allow the Lord Advocate to accept a compromise and safeguard the place of religious instruction in Scottish schools. Gordon was a strong churchman always anxious to see the Established Church and the Free Church reconciled. Two years later, in 1874, he would help to draft the Bill abolishing patronage. At the beginning of May 1872 Gordon proposed that there should be a clause in the Bill which would secure religious education in schools by "use and wont": "Having regard to the principles and history of the past educational legislation and practice of Scotland, which provides for instruction in the Holy Scriptures as an essential part of education, this House, while desirous of passing a measure during the present session for improvement of education in Scotland, is of the opinion that the law and practice of Scotland in this respect should be continued by provisions in the bill now before the House."[15]

Gordon had considerable support in the Commons and had been responsible for bringing in the Scottish Reform Bill in 1868. He reminded the House that in the past year there had been 903 petitions against the Bill praying for alterations with a view to securing religious instruction as it had always existed in Scottish schools. Reluctant to speak against the Liberal government under Prime Minister Gladstone and in support of an opposition motion, the Scottish Liberals, since the 1868 Reform Act the strongest party in Scotland, said little during the debate and were accused of being unwilling to defend the system of education which the Scottish people desired, and in the end Gordon's amendment was carried by a majority of only seven. His amendment was then taken up in the Lords by the Duke of Richmond who proposed inserting a clause in the Preamble stating that religious instruction, "as an essential part of education," should be given to all children whose parents did not decline it on religious grounds. Opposing him Argyll argued that religious teaching would be continued in Scotland by local boards just as well as it would be if left in the hands of Presbyteries or Bishops but Richmond's amendment was carried in the Lords by a majority of twenty-one. When the amended Bill went back to the Commons in July the Lord Advocate refused to accept

15. Scottish Education Bill Report of Parliamentary Debate on Mr Gordon's Resolution in Favour of "Instruction in the Holy Scriptures in the Public Schools," adopted by House of Commons on Monday Evening, 6th May, 1872 [Hansard 3rd Series CCXI 288].

the new insertion but proposed altering it to read: "Whereas it has been the custom in the public schools of Scotland to give instruction in religion to children whose parents did not object to the instruction so given, but with liberty to parents without forfeiting any of the other advantages . . . to elect that their children should not receive such instruction, and it is expedient that the managers of public schools shall be at liberty to continue the said custom: Be it therefore enacted."[16] Gordon reluctantly agreed to this version and it was passed at a poorly attended evening session by 113 votes to 5. Important as this amendment to the Preamble was, it did not in the end achieve what Gordon had wanted. It left the matter still very open and it did not guarantee that religious instruction would be taught according to the "use and wont" of Scottish schools. Indeed in some schools for a time after 1872 no formal religious instruction was given but this was the exception. Nevertheless, the fact that even the possibility of giving religious instruction was enshrined in legislation, would remain of great importance for the Church of Scotland in the twentieth century. The 1980 Education (Scotland) Act strengthened the position of religious instruction making it unlawful to discontinue it in a school unless this was approved by a majority of the electors concerned.

During the progress of the 1872 Bill the Church continued to try and influence the outcome. The debate at the General Assembly in May lasted till midnight. In particular there were anxieties about the future of religious instruction, the status and remuneration of teachers, and the control London might exert on any Scottish Board. Some felt that it would be acceptable to teach from the Bible as long no catechism or denominational creed or doctrine like the Westminster Confession was introduced. There was also some concern about the effect compulsory attendance might have on the poorer sections of the community where children would no longer be able to work and supplement the family income. To the end the Church maintained that the need of more schools was being exaggerated but now it contented itself with again pressing for the Bill to include those clauses of the English Education Act which provided that new school boards would only be set up where the educational needs of a community were not already being met. Had the government agreed to this the Established Church would have achieved its objective not only of retaining its own schools but also of ensuring the continua-

---

16. See Appendix 5.1 for further details of the Preamble.

tion of existing parish schools with their traditional Church connection. The Church had always objected strongly to Scottish education being run from Whitehall, and such an arrangement would have limited the control of any Central Board to the new National schools. Young, however, was not prepared to make any more concessions and certainly not one like this which would have played into the hands of Disraeli and the Conservatives by perpetuating the power of the heritors and the landed class in the old parish boards, and the Bill was passed on 2 August.

LEARNING AND TEACHING IN CHURCH SCHOOLS (1864–1872)

Church Funding

In the climate of uncertainty created by the Argyll Commission's inquiries and the subsequent Bills on Scottish education, the Established Church's Education Committee persevered in its efforts to extend and improve schooling throughout the country. It was determined to prove to the government that any gaps in the system could be met by extending the voluntary sector. It is somewhat ironic that, in the years immediately prior to the transfer of responsibility for Church schools to local boards under the 1872 Act, the Education Committee's income from congregations showed greater annual increases than had been the case for many years. By 1870 the Church had sufficient funding to raise teachers' salaries, improve school buildings in the Highlands, and offer to build new schools wherever they were required.

Of course the committee did not hesitate to use the current Education Bills and the threat of new National schools to pressure congregations into supporting its schools. In 1864 the committee was paying out £3,300 for the support of its 202 Assembly schools. By 1871 the number of Assembly schools had increased to 286.[17] The Church also took credit for managing over 120 Sewing schools and for the education of 2,000 pupils who were attending Sabbath schools instead of week-day schools. In 1866 it reported that over the previous three years it had been able to

17. The exact number of schools funded one way or another by the Church of Scotland is very difficult to calculate. It may include Assembly schools, SSPCK schools, Sessional and congregational schools, schools founded and endowed by Church members such as Public works and Heritors' schools and Sewing Schools. The numbers quoted in reports and by historians differ according to the categories included. The Reports of Presbyteries on Schools, December 1872, gives 1250 as the number of schools "which owe their existence to the voluntary exertions of ministers and members of the Church."

meet all expenditure on Female Schools from private subscriptions and it was confidently expected that there would be further funds to expand this work. By 1867 the funds were showing a healthy balance of some £10,000 hence the claim made to the Argyll Commission that the Church was in a position to extend its operations. It is no wonder that the committee felt that it would be a matter of regret if its work should be curtailed at the height of its success.

Teachers and Curriculum

In all its protestations against changes to the educational system, the Church was most adamant that the salaries and status of teachers should be protected. It argued that the higher the minimum salary, the better would be the quality of the teachers. It believed that well trained and qualified teachers were necessary if the tradition of elementary education leading directly to higher education was to be continued and it sought to pursue this policy within its own schools. In 1867 the committee reported that over the last ten years the number of teachers in receipt of the Privy Council's Certificate of Merit had risen from 33 percent to 60 percent indicating an improvement both in the efficiency of the teachers and in the quality of school accommodation. Over the ten years from 1862 to 1872 the average salary of certificated male teachers in Assembly schools increased from £58 to about £70, for females it rose from £38 to £50. (Uncertificated teachers in 1871 received £37.) This increase brought Assembly school teachers up to about the same level as teachers in parish schools and helped to reduce the drain of teachers from Church schools to parish schools. Encouraged by government policy the Church continued to recruit female teachers and increase the number of female schools. Some of these recruits were sewing mistresses but many were assistant teachers who took their share of the school curriculum. Often the female teacher was responsible for the infant department for a part of the day and for the industrial instruction of the senior girls at another time thus freeing up the schoolmaster to promote the more advanced classes in Latin and Mathematics. The only fear was that the time would come when the government might try to save money by insisting that Mistresses should be substituted for Masters in elementary schools.

In June 1864 the Committee of Council took the decision not to apply the Revised Code to Scottish schools pending the results of the Argyll

Commission. Nevertheless, inspectors were directed to inspect schools and examine pupils according to the instructions of the Revised Code. The initial results of these inspections showed that, compared to England, the grant-aided schools in Scotland were inferior in Writing and Arithmetic, but in neither country was the standard satisfactory. In Scotland: almost 11 percent failed the test in Reading, over 28 percent failed in Writing, and over 33 percent failed in Arithmetic. By 1865–6 Scotland came out better than England and there was a considerable improvement in the results— the number failing in Reading was reduced to 5 percent, in Writing to 13 percent, and in Arithmetic to 21 percent. According to the commissioners this was due to the stimulus of the Revised Code system of examination and even the Education Committee, noting the increase in instruction in the 3Rs, grudgingly admitted that the country was indebted partly to the instruction given to students in the Training Colleges, but mainly to the Revised Code. The committee, however, continued to maintain that this concentration on reading, writing, and arithmetic might be appropriate in England but was likely to have an adverse effect on the higher branches of education in Scotland. Undaunted by those who had denigrated the value of their contributions, the presbyteries of the Established Church continued to visit schools of every description throughout the land and the Education Committee carefully collated their reports and presented them to the General Assembly. As well as indicating where it was necessary to take any action required in Church schools, these reports when published provided the nation with an insight into the state of both parish and non-parish schools. The report to the 1869 Assembly, for example, revealed that in parish schools, in spite of the influence of the Revised Code with its emphasis on elementary subjects, the number learning Latin, Greek, French, and German showed an increase. Assembly schools continued to concentrate on the elementary subjects but from time to time exceptions to the rule were noted especially in the rural areas. In Lochinver where only seven pupils out of forty-eight managed to put in more than 150 attendances in a year, ten were learning Latin, while at Lochcarron Female School where only forty-one out of 128 attended 150 days or more, eleven of the girls were learning Latin and six mathematics.

Teacher Training

Although not fully operational in schools, the Revised Code was applied to the funding arrangements for Normal schools. Under the new scheme the Church's teacher training scheme was no longer subsidized through scholarships and capitation grants for teachers in training, instead the Church was paid only for the number of teachers who completed two years at college and two years teaching in an elementary school. Since not all who attended a Normal school ended up having completed two years, the Church protested that it would always be out of pocket. So serious was the position that at its meeting in 1864 the General Assembly was informed that the very existence of the Normal schools was at risk and the Assembly even went so far as to give powers to the Education Committee to close one or both of its Normal schools if that became necessary. The uncertainty created by all this meant that fewer came forward as pupil-teachers and there were fewer applicants for Normal schools. In spite of this, recruitment continued to equal the demand. The cash-flow problem remained, however, and the committee appealed to parish ministers to help place new teachers as quickly as possible since government funding was not recoverable until they had served two years teaching in schools.

In December 1871 the Church's teacher training programme received yet another blow. It was informed by the Education Department in London that the religious instruction course would no longer be prescribed by the Privy Council for students in training colleges, thus jeopardizing the already endangered place of religious instruction in schools. When presented with those Education Bills which threatened to remove religious instruction from the school curriculum, the committee had consistently argued that the Privy Council had made the provision of religious education in Normal schools one of the conditions for funding. Now this plank was being removed from under it. What was being proposed seemed to contradict all that had been agreed with the Privy Council under the existing Code. The justification given was that the change had had to be made for England in terms of its Education Act, and it was assumed that the same principle would be affirmed in the coming Education (Scotland) Act. When the committee protested the Committee of Council replied that "the principles affirmed by Parliament in the English Education Act, as to the payment of Privy Council grants on account of secular subjects only, *were substantially, if not formally,*

Imperial in their reference, and not merely applicable to England" (my italics).[18] This high-handed approach did nothing to endear the Church to any new London-controlled Scottish Education Department which might be proposed. The committee's protests that there had been no consultation were in vain. They were advised by the Vice-President of the Council to accept the situation or the Church might lose all Government maintenance grants for Training Colleges. Ultimately the Church made its own arrangements for keeping religious instruction on the Normal school curriculum and the 1872 Act did not affect the training colleges which remained under Church control.

18. Education Committee Report, 1871, Appendix III, 51.

Appendix 5.1

EXTRACTS FROM THE PREAMBLE TO EDUCATION
(SCOTLAND ACT) 1872

1. And whereas it has been the custom in the public schools of Scotland to give instruction in religion to children whose parents did not object to the instruction so given, but with liberty to parents, without forfeiting any of the other advantages of the schools, to elect that their children should not receive such instruction, and it is expedient that the managers of public schools should be at liberty to continue the said custom.

2. Every public school, and every school subject to inspection and in receipt of any public money as herein-before provided, shall be open to children of all denominations, and any child may be withdrawn by his parents from any instruction in religious subjects and from any religious observance in such school, and no child in any such school be placed at any disadvantage with respect to the secular instruction given therein by reason of the denomination to which such child or his parents belong, by reason of his being withdrawn from any instruction in religious subjects. The time or times during which any religious observance is practised or instruction in religious subjects is given at any meeting of the school for elementary instruction shall be either at the beginning or at the end, or at the beginning and at the end of such meeting and shall be specified in a table to be approved by the Scotch Education department.

6

A Vision Fulfilled

THE OUTCOME OF THE 1872 EDUCATION (SCOTLAND) ACT

THE EDUCATION (SCOTLAND) ACT of 1872 remains one of the milestones in the history of Scottish school education. It completed the secularization of school education which had been begun with the Act of 1861 by finally transferring the full control of schools from church to state. The Board of Education for Scotland and later the Scotch Education Department set up by the Act, however, was heavily weighted in terms of English input and was based in London. The Lord President and the Vice-President of the Privy Council acted as chief executives in both the English and the Scottish Departments and the same Permanent Secretary was secretary to both. This London connection lasted till 1885 when the Scottish Education Department was made independent. As we have seen the Act made no provision for funding secondary education, furthermore while insisting that teachers should have a certificate of proficiency, it made no provision for their training and left the professional preparation of teachers to the churches. It is to the credit of the churches training colleges (formerly called Normal schools) that by 1883 only one teacher in four was completely untrained.

Another result of the change to a London-based education authority which had a long-term effect on Scottish culture was the use of Gaelic in Scottish schools. There is no mention of Gaelic schools or the different linguistic needs of the Highlands and Islands in the 1872 Act. Schools managed by the Church and other organizations such as the SSPCK had been sympathetic to the use of Gaelic alongside English in their schools but after 1872 these became parish schools and were managed by the new school boards. The use of Gaelic was unofficially but actively discouraged and children were sometimes physically punished for speaking Gaelic in school. The SSPCK soon closed its schools down and the schools set up by the Gaelic Schools Society soon disappeared. The situation was complicated, however, as many of the Highlanders themselves were opposed to Gaelic as an educational language believing that learning English opened more doors to professions and occupations.

That George Young succeeded where Moncreiff and Argyll had failed was partly due to Young's personality. He was not one to seek compromises. His management of Scotland has been described as autocratic and masterful. The passing of such a revolutionary Act, however, also had a lot to do with the changing nature and relationships of the Presbyterian churches in Scotland. The Free Church and the Established Church had been willing to sacrifice their schools in order to safeguard the position of religious instruction. Altogether in the churches there was now less acrimonious competition, less interest in denominational self-preservation and more interest in reunion. There were conversations between the Free Church and the United Presbyterians. These two churches would come together as the United Free Church in 1900. The Kirk was willing to surrender patronage for good and there were indications that it was becoming more open to theological questioning and less bound by the Westminster Confession. All these moves produced a climate of opinion which made the 1872 Act more acceptable to the churches. Some historians, for example Drummond and Bulloch,[1] have attributed the passing of 1872 Act as the result of a weak Church succumbing to the inevitable. On the contrary as we noted in a previous chapter recent research by C. G. Brown now seems to indicate that levels of church attendance were not as bad as previous historians have claimed: "It seems clear to most specialists in the field that the levels of churchgoing revealed in the 1851 religious census were historically very high—in Scotland the figures were marginally higher than in England despite a markedly high number of non-returns from enumerators . . . despite the problems with the data, it is possible to say with reasonable certainty that church membership per capita grew from the 1840s to reach a peak in England and Wales in 1904 and in Scotland in 1905."[2]

1. Drummond and Bulloch, *The Church in Late Victorian Scotland*, 167.
2. Brown, *The Death of Christian Britain*, 161–63.

The old Moderate Party had found new blood in men like Norman MacLeod, Robert Lee, and Archibald Charteris, who had all contributed to stimulating popular interest in the Church. The notion of a weak Church, moreover, takes no account of the increasing willingness to cooperate shown by the different denominations. The fact that reunion was being discussed and the Creeds and Confessions re-examined was a sign of strength and not of weakness, of looking forward and not of retrenchment. In response to the Argyll Commission's assertion that the permanence of denominational schools was precarious, the Church pointed out that the number of Assembly Schools was on the increase and that it was well able to fund them. Even the Society in Scotland for Propagating Christian Knowledge was coping financially. It may have been rash of the Church to claim that, had parish system been continued, it could have coped with the educational needs of the country. Nonetheless, it cannot be denied that in the early 1870s the financial position of the Education Committee was as strong as it had ever been.

The 1872 Act did not outlaw denominational schools. However, its legislation for rate-supported schools throughout the land did make the Church of Scotland's schools more or less superfluous. The Church could not have expected its members to pay for the new schools through the rates and also contribute through collections and donations to Assembly schools. The only reason for keeping Church schools would have been to secure religious instruction. In a Memorandum issued by the Education Committee shortly after the passing of the Act, the Convener, John Cook, pointed out that the Church found itself in a difficult situation because from the start many of its schools such as those financed by heritors and manufacturers and kirk sessions had never been strictly denominational since they had been established to meet the educational needs of the country and not to propagate any particular religious teaching. Within the next few years, however, it was apparent that congregational contributions for Assembly schools was decreasing and the Church began to hand over the management of its schools to the local boards and these boards, despite the Church's fears, proved willing to allow religious instruction its traditional place in the school curriculum as laid down in the Preamble to the 1872 Act. In 1878 a school inspector included this statement in his report: "The religious question engrosses men's minds no longer. For the present it is no more a rock of difficulty . . . The boards, with surprising uniformity of action, or rather inaction, practically left the subject in the position in which they found it. They settled it everywhere and in every case on its traditional basis. They simply stereotyped and enforced the hereditary *status quo,* or what is termed 'use and wont.'"[3]

The Established Church continued to have considerable influence in school education until well into the twentieth century. Of the 5,662 members elected to the first boards formed after the passing of the Act, 1,450 were clergymen, among them 744 Established Church ministers. Moreover, although the Church lost control of schools under the 1872 Act, teacher training colleges remained under its control until 1907. The General Assembly's Education Committee established in 1825 continues to monitor state education, contribute to the relevant political discussions, and support Religious and Moral Education in schools. The Church still appoints someone to represent it on local authority education committees. As we have noted above it is now unlawful for an education authority to discontinue religious education unless the proposal to do so has been the subject of a poll of the local government electors in the area concerned and has been approved by the majority of those voters. Denominational schools, mainly Roman Catholic, are funded in the same way as are non-denominational schools and are open to pupils of all denominations.

THE ACHIEVEMENTS OF THE CHURCH OF SCOTLAND

In 1824 moved by the desperate need for schools in the Highlands and Islands and inspired by the Reformers' vision of a school in every parish the Church of Scotland had set out to establish a scheme of national education under its control. In implementing its education programme in the nineteenth century, the Church saw itself as fulfilling an obligation that had been passed on to it by Knox and the Reformers. It regarded the parish school system as part of a legacy handed down and believed that the Act of Union had confirmed it as the rightful heir. The Church's education policy in the nineteenth century reflected its belief that it was preserving a tradition which, in the spirit of the *First Book of Discipline,* brought together a spiritual and a secular education and that this was accomplished through teachers being members of the Established Church. The Church, accordingly, pursued a system which promoted the educa-

3. This Report was quoted in a Scottish Education Department Memorandum, published in February 1943: *Memorandum with regard to the provision made for Religious Instruction in the Schools in Scotland* (Cmd. 6426, Edinburgh: His Majesty's Stationery Office, 1943), 6.

tion of the whole person. Education offered preparation for life in this world and the next. At a time when no nation-wide authority existed to foster and manage a system of education the Church succeeded. It developed a system which was without parallel in Europe, except perhaps in Germany, and paved the way for the 1872 Act.

Certainly there were times when the importance of religious instruction seemed to dominate but it would be wrong to believe that the curriculum followed either in parish schools or in Assembly schools was mainly to proselytize. Even the most basic education in the three Rs offered by Assembly schools gave people a sense of worth and an opportunity to make the most of their lives. The Education Committee did believe, however, that a knowledge of the Bible and instruction in the Shorter Catechism were necessary to the formation of the national character and for the good of the "Commonwealth." It is to be regretted that the prominence given to religious instruction by the Church in its public statements and reports during the 1850s and 1860s, has diverted attention from its overall contribution to education in these decades. In fact it is to the Education Committee's credit that it set out to maintain the best traditions in Scottish education. In keeping with the *First Book of Discipline*'s ideal the Church attempted to provide a system which was both democratic and meritocratic. Indeed, it was to encourage those who up until then had had little chance of any education that the committee pursued its policies in those areas which were either geographically or socially the most disadvantaged. Compared to similar schools in England Scottish parish schools and Assembly schools drew from a wider social spectrum, offered a broader curriculum, and even enabled talented students to go to university. The Argyll Commission found that in the 1860s in Scottish universities there was at least one matriculated student for every 1,000 of the population. In England it was one in every 5,800 and in Germany 1 in every 2,600. The Church opened its schools to all irrespective of social status and encouraged a policy of tolerance towards parents who objected to the type of religious instruction being taught. How many children with ability from poorer working-class backgrounds (the "lads o' pairts") actually made it to university and into the professions may be debatable and must always have depended not just on the standard of education but on the regularity of school attendance. In a survey conducted by the Argyll Commission on the professions and occupations of the fathers of 882 of the students in the Latin, Greek, and Mathematics classes in the

Universities of Edinburgh, Glasgow, and St Andrews, and of the Junior Latin and Greek classes in Aberdeen (Session 1866–1867), it found that 31 percent of the students came from professional backgrounds (teachers, lawyers, ministers, engineers, army officers etc.), 18 percent came from agricultural backgrounds and 16 percent came from artisan and laboring backgrounds (builders, blacksmiths, joiners, masons, plumbers, etc.)[4] The fact is that the Church's policy made access to university more likely than it would otherwise have been. The opportunities were there but were always not taken up.

There were many indications of the Church's commitment to good secular education. In keeping with its democratic ideal the Church operated on the principle that all boys should have every opportunity to prepare themselves for future employment and for further education and developed a wide ranging curriculum to that end. In almost all Church schools as well as religious instruction the curriculum included Reading, Writing, Arithmetic, Geography, and Grammar and in many others pupils were encouraged to study History, Mensuration, Book-keeping, Geometry, Algebra, Latin, Greek, French, German, Music, and Drawing. The Education Committee, moreover, took advantage of government grants to extend its interest in vocational subjects—in female education, sewing schools, and in agricultural and industrial schools—which it regarded as necessary for any permanent improvement in the condition of the people. Many from working-class backgrounds were able to go on and further their education at the new Mechanics' Institutes and Evening Schools which were burgeoning at this time and which were offering a fairly comprehensive curriculum.

Though not always happy with the conditions and regulations that came with government funding, the committee persuaded the Church that this was the way forward and that by accepting grants the educational work could be advanced without the Church's religious freedom being compromised. Indeed, by the 1860s there was a body of opinion within the Church in favor of a national scheme and had Argyll's Bill reflected more faithfully the findings and recommendations of the Royal Commission, the Church might well have been persuaded to accept it. In its movement towards the acceptance of a national system of education, the Church was no doubt latterly influenced by the growing numbers in

4. Argyll Commission, *Third Report, Report of the Assistant-Commissioners on the State of Education in the Burgh and Middle-Class schools in Scotland*, 237–42.

what has been described as the "Broad Church" group. This comprised university teachers and churchmen such as John Caird and John Tulloch, who took a more liberal and critical approach to the Bible and to the Westminster Confession and who may not have regarded the teaching of the Catechism and the orthodoxy of the schoolmasters as principles that had to be defended at all costs.

To achieve its ends the Church of Scotland continually tried to raise the qualifications of teachers. Early on the Education Committee saw the need for professional teacher training with its emphasis not only on academic ability but also on the necessary pedagogical skills. Its Normal schools were among the first in the United Kingdom and led the way in providing instruction in "the art of teaching." In spite of the financial struggle involved, in co-operation with the Parliamentary Privy Council Committee, the Church continued to extend and upgrade its training colleges, providing Scotland with well qualified teachers throughout the nineteenth century. As more parish and Assembly teachers gained government Certificates of Merit, their chances of government salary augmentations improved. In this way at least the Church helped to advance the lot of schoolmasters. It is true that the Church's disciplinary procedures with regard to teachers had long been challenged and its power in this respect was certainly curtailed by the Education Act of 1861. Presbytery examinations had not always been efficient or effective and as the curriculum expanded and as good teaching practice became more important, government inspectors were better qualified than ministers to assess proficiency. All this, however, should not detract from the fact that the Church was the pioneer of school inspection. It recognized that if there was to be any improvement in standards then there had to be some named person or persons to visit and some body like the General Assembly with an overview of the situation. This annual examination may well have motivated teachers and pupils and helped to promote higher academic and moral standards among teachers. Moreover, the Church was quick to recognize that if standards were to improve Scottish education needed government funding even if this meant accepting the state inspection of schools that came with it.

Following the Disruption, many believed that an educational system based on the principle of government-supported denominational schools contributed to sectarianism. This was certainly the view of those who believed that the parish schools should no longer be under the control of the

Established Church. Bodies such as the National Education Association of Scotland held up the Edinburgh High School as an example of a national non-sectarian school where the local board of patrons consisted of men of all sects and parties and teachers belonged to the Episcopalian, Presbyterian, and Dissenting denominations. Those who argued for a non-denominational national system used "denominationalism" and "sectarianism" almost synonymously, "sect" being used in a pejorative sense implying bigotry and division. The Church, as might have been expected, saw the situation differently. It did not regard denominationalism as implying sectarianism nor did it consider its control of parish schools as responsible for any animosity that might exist in the community since it admitted the children of any religious body to its schools. This was certainly borne out by the Argyll Commission's findings. There we find that of 33,251 pupils on the rolls of Church of Scotland schools, only 18,020 belonged to the Church of Scotland (54 percent) while over 33 percent belonged either to the Free Church or to the United Presbyterian Church. Similarly more than a fifth of pupils attending Free Church schools belonged to the Church of Scotland. While by the time of the Argyll Report (1867) 61 Catholic schools and 74 Episcopalian schools had been established, still almost 20 percent of all Catholic pupils and 18 percent of all Episcopalian pupils went either to Church of Scotland schools or to parish schools supervised by the Church. The huge social and economic changes in the Scotland which had resulted in widespread migration and immigration and urban expansion had resulted in a mushrooming of schools to meet the needs of the time—charitable schools, private schools, schools located in mining and industrial towns established by employers, girls' schools—all this alongside schools set up by different denominations. In spite of this the statistics reveal that almost 39 percent of all pupils attending schools in Scotland attended parish schools or Church of Scotland schools, indicating that the people of Scotland still had confidence in the Church and its continued interest in parish schools irrespective of its opinions on the proposed schemes for a national system of education. Granted such statistics may also say something about the availability and proximity of schooling, nevertheless they do show that parents' desire to do the best for their children came before any sectarian feelings they may have had.

In recalling the importance of the Act of Union and the statutory responsibility conferred on it, the Church believed that education had an important contribution to make to Scotland's nationhood. The importance of a spirit of nationalism in Scotland in the nineteenth century is still a matter of debate among historians. Some have believed that the failure of the early attempts to change the education system exposed Scotland to anglicizing influences. After the Disruption the Church of Scotland found itself in an awkward position on this issue. It looked to the Act of Union to uphold its claim to be the Established Church, it depended on British government grants and very often it relied on the support of English Conservative MPs to defeat the education bills promoted by the Liberals which would have undermined its authority in the management and supervision of parish schools. On the other hand, in its opposition to many of the changes that were being proposed by the Privy Council and education reformers—the introduction of pupil teachers, the funding arrangements for its education colleges, the Revised Code's emphasis on the three Rs and the centralization of authority in an Education Board in London—the Church showed an awareness of the threat of assimilation to the English scheme. Influential Free Church ministers like James Begg and Thomas Guthrie who were in favor of a national system of education were also supporters of movements such as the National Education Association of Scotland and the National Association for the Vindication of Scottish Rights which were indications of an embryonic nationalist movement. The fact that revision of the English education system was being considered at the same time in Parliament did not help the Church of Scotland in its attempts to have the Scottish situation treated independently. The debates in presbyteries and in the General Assembly over the acceptance of government inspection as a condition for receiving Privy Council funding and the agreement to take government augmentation for Assembly teachers' salaries even when those of parish schoolmasters were held down because the government refused to recognize the heritors' financial support as "voluntary contributions", illustrated the Church's dilemma. The more dependent the Church became on government funding for its training colleges and Assembly schools, the weaker were its arguments for refusing to become part of a new national system in Scotland. In 1845 the Poor Law Amendment Act had taken responsibility for poor relief out of the hands of the Church and placed it with a central board of supervision and organized it according to the practice in England. In the same year Scottish banking was remodeled on the English system and Scottish banks had to struggle to retain their own identity. In the light of such changes the Church's unwillingness to relinquish its hold on parish schools in the 1850s and 1860s, might have been regarded merely as a show of strength in the face of rival denominations but from the Church's point of view it was seen as a way of being consistent in its role as the preserver of an educational tradition that had shaped the fabric of Scottish life. The Kirk, however, could not stem the tide of the political and religious changes which were undermining its efforts. William Storrar in his examination of Scottish identity argues that:

> In the mid-nineteenth century the Scottish Reformed tradition and vision of the nation underwent a historic failure of theological and intellectual nerve . . . the new urban working class with its large Irish Catholic and unchurched elements, the British State, governing according to alien Anglican and erastian constitutional norms, the numerically comparable Presbyterian seceders, calling for disestablishment of the Kirk . . . all these groups and many more were indifferent or hostile to the Church of Scotland. They rejected its spiritual responsibility for the whole nation. They ignored its historic role as the key institution generating and guaranteeing a common sense of Scottish identity.[5]

Within the limitations of its powers and resources, the Education Committee's achievements were remarkable. When John Gordon, a former secretary to the Church of Scotland Education Committee, gave evidence before the Argyll Commission in November 1864, he described the object of the Church's education scheme as "to supply schools for elementary instruction in those parts of Scotland in which, from local causes, schools have been wanting; that is mainly in the Highlands." In fulfillment of this objective the Church, in co-operation with the SSPCK (reckoned by the Argyll Commission to be maintaining 202 schools) had set about tackling the problems of literacy in Gaelic-speaking areas and had set up schools in the remote glens of the Highlands and Islands and in the deprived communities of the industrial Lowlands. Between 1825 and 1871 the Church, with the help of congregational donations and individual endowments, established 286 Assembly schools, over 135 Sessional schools and numerous Public Works and Trust schools.[6] In numbers alone, the Church had made an important contribution to Scottish school education. Gordon's description of the Church of Scotland's objective, however, did not do

5. Storrar, *Scottish Identity: A Christian Vision*, 47.

6. The statistics are taken from the *Education Committee Report*, 1871.

justice to the wider programme in which the Church was involved. In establishing its new schools, the Church saw itself as supplementing an existing system of national education for which it had a statutory managerial responsibility. In a response to the Argyll Commission's Report, the Education Committee convener, John Cook, anxious to repudiate the commission's statement that a supplementary system had been "forced into existence partly by denominational rivalry," observed that more than half of the Assembly schools, 146, had been set up before the Disruption.[7] In its published statistics the committee always included parish schools as "Church of Scotland schools." In 1871, including 1,200 parish schools, the Church claimed responsibility for a total of 2,430 schools throughout the country.[8] By the 1860s so many new schools had been erected that both the Church of Scotland and the Free Church agreed that the main problem was not the lack of schools, rather it was with issues with which only government legislation could deal—school attendance, deficient buildings, and teachers' salaries.

In its support of an education system which emphasized both the secular and the religious responsibilities of schools, the Church saw itself as faithfully continuing a tradition established by the Scottish reformers. Where it succeeded, it did so by being prepared at times to stand by its beliefs and at other times, by being politic and being prepared to compromise when necessary. By accepting state aid and government inspection it helped to lay the foundations for a national state-supported system in Scotland with schooling available throughout the land and elementary education made compulsory, as Knox had planned. In so doing it could rightly claim to have seen "a vision fulfilled."

7. Cook seems to have ignored the fact that denominational rivalry had existed long before the Disruption, provoked in particular as the United Secession Church (Voluntaries) grew in strength.

8. According to an 1871 Education Committee Report, this number takes account of "schools in connection with the General Assembly's Education Committee, the Society for Propagating Christian Knowledge, Public Works, Kirk-sessions, Trusts, Congregations, and individual heritors—numbering in all about 1200 institutions."

Selected Bibliography

Argyll Commission Reports 1865–1868, (Edinburgh; Thomas Constable for H. M. Stationery Office) University of Edinburgh Moray House.

Church of Scotland Synod, Presbytery, and Kirk Session Minutes in the National Archives of Scotland.

Free Church of Scotland Assembly Proceedings, 1843–1850.

~

Anderson R. D. *Education and the Scottish People, 1750–1918.* Oxford: Clarendon, 1995.

Baird, George H. *Extracts from reports of the ministers of parishes in some synods of Scotland: made in 1818 and 1819, as to parochial schools.* Edinburgh: Duncan Stevenson, 1824.

Belford, A. J. *Centenary Handbook of the Educational Institute of Scotland.* Edinburgh: The Educational Institute of Scotland, 1946.

Brims, John D. "The Scottish Jacobins; Scottish Nationalism and the British Union." In *Scotland and England, 1286–1815,* edited by R. A. Mason, 247–65. Edinburgh: Donald, 1987.

Brown, Callum G. *The Death of Christian Britain: Understanding Secularisation: 1800–2000.* Christianity and Society in the Modern World. London: Routledge, 2001.

———. "Religion and Social Change." In *People and Society in Scotland, 1760–1830,* edited by T. M. Devine and Rosalind Mitchison, 143–62. People and Society in Scotland 1. Edinburgh: Donald, 1988.

———. *Religion and Society in Scotland since 1707.* Rev. ed. Edinburgh: Edinburgh University Press, 1997.

———. *The Social History of Religion in Scotland since 1730.* Christianity and Society in the Modern World. London: Methuen, 1987.

———. "The Sunday School Movement in Scotland, 1780–1914." *Records of the Scottish Church History Society* 21 (1981) 3–26.

Brown, Stewart J. *Thomas Chalmers and the Godly Commonwealth in Scotland.* Oxford: Oxford University Press, 1982.

Bryce, James. *Public Education in Relation to Scotland and Its Parish Schools: A Letter to the Rt. Hon. the Earl of Aberdeen.* Edinburgh: Blackwood, 1854.

Cameron, James K., editor. *The First Book of Discipline.* Edinburgh: Saint Andrew, 1972.

Camic, Charles. *Experience and Enlightenment: Socialization for Cultural Change in Eighteenth-Century Scotland.* Edinburgh: Edinburgh University Press, 1983.

Campbell, Andrew J. *Two Centuries of the Church of Scotland 1707–1929.* Paisley: Gardner, 1930.

Devine, T. M. *The Scottish Nation, 1700–2000.* Harmondsworth: Penguin, 2000.

Drummond, Andrew L., and James Bulloch. *The Church in Late Victorian Scotland 1874–1900.* Edinburgh: Saint Andrew, 1978.

————. *The Church in Victorian Scotland 1843–1874*. Edinburgh: St. Andrew, 1975.

Dwyer, John. *Virtuous Discourse: Sensibility and Community in Late Eighteenth-Century Scotland*. Edinburgh: Donald, 1987.

Galt, John. *Annals of the Parish; The Ayrshire Legatees; The Provost*. Edinburgh: The Saltire Society, 2002.

General Assembly of the Church of Scotland, Acts and Proceedings of General Assembly, Education Committee Reports, University of Edinburgh New College Library.

Gillis, James. *A Letter to the Rt. Hon. Duncan Maclaren, on the proposed "Voluntary" Amendment of the Lord Advocate's Education Bill for Scotland*. Edinburgh: Marsh & Beattie, 1854.

Guthrie, Thomas. *Report of the Proceedings at the Public Meeting of the Friends of National Education in The Music Hall, Edinburgh*, January 1854. Edinburgh: Black, 1854.

————. *The Scotch Education Bill: A Letter from Dr. Guthrie to my Fellow Countrymen*. Edinburgh: Greig & Son, 1872.

Hansard Parliamentary Debates, 3rd series, vols. 68, 82, 97, 98, 100, 163, 164, 194, 196, 211, and 212.

Hetherington W. M. *National Education in Scotland Viewed in Its Present Condition, Its Principles, and Its Possibilities*. 2nd ed. Edinburgh: Johnstone & Hunter, 1850.

Kyd, James Gray, editor. *Scottish Population Statistics, Including Webster's Analysis of Population, 1755*. Publications of the Scottish History Society, 3rd Series, 44. Edinburgh: Scottish History Society, 1952.

Law, Alexander. *Edinburgh Schools of the Nineteenth Century*. Edinburgh: n.p., 1995.

Lockhart, J. G. *Peter's Letters to His Kinsfolk*. Vol. 3. 3 vols. 3rd ed. Edinburgh: Blackwood, 1819.

MacLeod, Norman. *Reminiscences of a Highland Parish*. London: Partridge, n.d.

Main, Archibald. "The Church and Education in the Eighteenth Century." *Records of the Scottish Church History Society* 3 (1929) n.p.

Mechie, Stewart. *The Church and Scottish Social Development, 1780–1870*. The Cunningham Lectures, 1957. London: Oxford University Press, 1960.

Miller, Hugh. *My Schools and Schoolmasters, Or, the Story of My Education*. Edited and introduced by James Robertson. Edinburgh: B. & W., 1993.

Moncreiff, James. *Speech of the Lord Advocate of Scotland in the House of Commons, Feb. 23, 1854, on the Bill for the Education of the People of Scotland*. London: Longman, Brown, Green, and Longmans, 1854.

Myers, J. D. "Scottish Nationalism and the Antecedents of the 1872 Education Act." *Scottish Educational Studies* 4 (May 1972) 73–92.

National Archives of Scotland (NAS) AD56, 47/3 and 47/4.

Omond, G. W. T. *The LordAdvocates of Scotland*. 2nd series, 1834-1880. London: Melrose, 1914.

Parliamentary Papers, Public Bills 186111I 7 June 1861 24 Viet., and 12 July 1861 24 & 25 Vict.

Peterkin, Alexander, editor. *The Booke of the Universal! Kirk of Scotland*. Edinburgh: The Edinburgh Printing and Publishing Co., 1839.

A Plea for the Parish Schools by a Parochial Schoolmaster. Edinburgh: Blackwood & Sons, 1867.

Proceedings of the United Presbyterian Church Synod, 1847–1850 and 1869.

"The Recommendations and Draft Bill: A Speech delivered by Mr Borrowman, of Auchtermuchty, at the Cupar Branch of the Educational Institute." *The Museum and English Journal of Education* 4 (1867) 415–16.

Scottish Education Department. *Memorandum with Regard to the Provision Made for Religious Instruction in the Schools in Scotland* (Cmd. 6426, Edinburgh: His Majesty's Stationery Office).

Scots Magazine, various volumes.

Sinclair, John, Sir. *Analysis of the Statistical Account of Scotland*. Part 2. London: Murray 1826.

———, editor. *The Old or First Statistical Account of Scotland*. 21 vols. Edinburgh: Creech, 1791–1799.

Smout, T. C. *A History of the Scottish People, 1560-1830*. Rev. ed. London: Fontana, 1972.

Society for the Benefit of the Sons and Daughters of the Clergy. *New Statistical Account of Scotland*. 15 vols. Edinburgh: Blackwood, 1845.

Somerville, Thomas. *My Own Life and Times, 1714-1814*. With a new introduction by Richard B. Sher. Scottish Thought and Culture, 1750–1800. Contemporary Memoirs. Bristol: Thoemmes, 1996.

Storrar, William. *Scottish Identity: A Christian Vision*. Edinburgh: Handsel, 1990.

Wilson, Thomas. "A Reinterpretation of 'Payment by Results' in Scotland, 1861–1872." In *Scottish Culture and Scottish Education, 1800-1980*, edited by Walter M. Humes and Hamish M. Paterson, 93–114. Edinburgh: Donald, 1983.

Withrington, Donald J. *Going to School: Scotland's Past in Action*. Edinburgh: National Museums of Scotland, 1997.

———. "The SPCK and Highland Schools in Mid-Eighteenth Century." *The Scottish Historical Review* 41 (1962).

Woodward, Llewellyn, Sir. *The Age of Reform, 1815-1870*. 2nd ed. Oxford: Clarendon, 1962.

Index